Please check all items for damages
before leaving the Library.
Thereafter you will be held
responsible for all injuries
to items beyond reasonable wear.

*Hannah
and the
Mountain*

American Lives

SERIES EDITOR
Tobias Wolff

HANNAH
and the Mountain

Notes toward
a Wilderness Fatherhood

Jonathan Johnson

UNIVERSITY OF NEBRASKA PRESS
LINCOLN & LONDON

© 2005 by the Board of Regents of the University of Nebraska

All rights reserved

Manufactured in the United States of America

⊗

Library of Congress Cataloging-in-Publication Data

Johnson, Jonathan, 1967–

Hannah and the mountain:

notes toward a

wilderness fatherhood / Jonathan Johnson.

224 p.   cm.   —(American lives)

ISBN 0-8032-2601-2 (cloth: alk. paper)

1. Johnson, Jonathan, 1967–Homes and haunts—Idaho.

2. Authors, American—20th century—Biography.

3. English teachers—United States—Biography.

4. Log cabins—Design and construction.

5. Wilderness areas—Idaho.

6. Married people—Idaho.

7. Fatherhood—Idaho.

8. Pregnancy—Idaho.

9. Idaho—Biography.

I. Title. II. Series.

PS3560.O37934Z465 2005

811'.6—dc22

2004015602

Epigraph to "Postpartum":

DONALD AND LYDIA, by John Prine

© 1971 (Renewed) Walden Music, Inc. & Sour Grapes Music

All Rights o/b/o Walden Music, Inc. administered by WB Music Corp.

All Rights Reserved   Used by Permission

WARNER BROS. PUBLICATIONS U.S. INC., Miami FL 33014

A portion of this book previously appeared as "The Calf"

in *Open Spaces* 3, no. 1 (2000): 5-8.

Designed and set in Stone Serif by R. W. Boeche.

Printed by Thomson-Shore, Inc.

This book is dedicated to Amy,
their mother

Contents

Acknowledgments   ix

The First Trimester   I

The Second Trimester   59

The Third Trimester   133

Postpartum   169

Acknowledgments

My deepest thanks to Rick Bass, Jennifer Bowman, Sharon Dilworth, Lee Gutkind, John Keeble, Carolyn Kremers, David Dodd Lee, and Russell Thorburn for advice and encouragement, and to Peter Markus for the inspiration. Thanks also to my agent, Tanya McKinnon, for her advocacy and essential editorial input.

Grateful acknowledgment is made to Penny Harrison, editor at *Open Spaces* magazine, where a portion of this book previously appeared under the title "The Calf."

The First
Trimester

You only have to let the soft animal
of your body love what it loves.

— Mary Oliver

A home pregnancy test sits on the windowsill. We sit on the edge of the bed, hunched over the woodstove in our coats and stocking hats. A light breeze ripples the plastic tacked over the openings where the windows will go. Pink dawn is rising over the mountain, first light falling on the most snow this valley has seen in fifty years of early Decembers.

Three minutes.

We hold each other and shiver, partly because the logs in the woodstove burned down to a little glowing pile of block-shaped coals while we slept last night, and partly because we are electrified, quivering with nervous energy as we wait. We make cold sounds, *brrr* and *oooh*, and rock together. I open the stove's heavy iron and glass door and toss in a couple pieces of split cedar. I close the door and slide open the damper, and in a few seconds the embers brighten, and a trace of yellow flame works its way up the spine of one of the sticks of fresh starter wood. The travel clock beside the bed reads 7:37.

Two minutes.

This is our first morning to wake up in the cabin, and it's my twenty-ninth birthday. We came up here with the pregnancy test last night, intending to find out then, to sit in the dark and watch the fire and listen to some music on our little, battery-powered stereo and contemplate the news.

Amy's known and it's been written all over her face for weeks. For weeks I've been falling in love with my wife all over again, looking at her in newly developed pictures of the previous week's cabin progress and seeing a mother, the green of water over river rocks in her eyes as she poses, holding a trowel, smiling up from where she's crouched to chink between two massive, dark tamarack logs, white chink smeared on her clothes and in the waves of her long, dark hair. We both knew. We bought the test just for confirmation. We gave ourselves last night, one last evening alone, kids ourselves, really, falling asleep beside the fire under mountains of quilts and blankets and sleeping bags, the pregnancy test unopened in its drugstore sack. We knew.

Or. Or what? Or we've both been fooling ourselves, Amy's body and both our minds concocting a beautiful fiction, trying on the idea of a baby crawling across the cabin floor, a baby sleeping in the sun in next summer's alfalfa.

Less than one minute.

The air in the cabin is cold, except for the small space around the stove where we've put our two chairs, our steamer trunk of clothes, and our mattress on the floor. The stillness is filled with the smells of sawdust and fiberglass insulation. Snow has drifted so high around us we couldn't see out of the kitchen even if we did have glass in the windows. The wall that will partition off the bathroom is nothing more than a skeleton of framed lumber. We have no water, no power, no phone, and our driveway winds a half-mile up through thick, steep woods. Often, after a storm, days pass before the plow comes. Never in my life have I felt so unprepared. And so ready.

Amy's not waiting. She gets up and walks over to the test on the windowsill and picks up the white strip in her wool mitten. Nothing moves. Not my heart, not the trace of flame in the stove, not the plastic on the windows. Not a single raven

4

in this valley leaves its branch; not a single branch gives up its snow in a silent, tiny cascade. When she turns around there are tears streaming down her cheeks. "I am so happy," she says and hands me the strip.

In one circle, for comparison, so there can be no mistake, is a pink stripe. Then, under clear plastic, bisecting the other white circle, pink! A pink line, blazing like the dawn above Butler Mountain.

We stand at the open door holding each other, listening for the echo of my ecstatic, top-of-my-lungs holler to return. There will be three of us.

Amy and I came to the mountains because our adult lives were rushing toward us and we wanted to go out and meet those lives in a place that would keep us young and free and filled with passion. After years of school we were ready to settle into the long story of home. We were overdue. If we wanted to begin that story surrounded by beauty, on land that would shape us with its years, we had to go now.

But our pilgrimage, when we finally got around to it, was roundabout. We moved to my family's ranch in Bonner County, Idaho, in August, after a summer spent sleeping in our tent and driving all over Alaska in our little old pickup, the back sagging from apple boxes full of books and dishes and winter clothes, as we searched for a landscape to trust our daydreams to. We'd driven all the way to the Arctic from Michigan, where we'd been living, but we never unpacked in Alaska.

First we tried Fairbanks, but Amy's a coastal dweller, having grown up on the shore of Lake Superior in Michigan's Upper Peninsula, and she had reservations about a life hundreds of miles from a beach. So I agreed to try the coast.

We found a cabin available for rent in a place called Fox River on the Kenai Peninsula. Then we walked the beach for hours, trying to decide if we should stay, should rent the Fox River cabin and make the Kenai Peninsula of Alaska ours. Amy stuffed sandy shells into her coat pockets as our big white dog, Yukon, ran, paws flopping, and jumped toward and away from the waves. We stood there, exhausted from weeks on the longest, dustiest, bumpiest road we'd ever driven, and watched the small halibut boats slip out toward Cook Inlet, the low sun skimming along glaciated mountains across Kachemak Bay. We were dazzled. We were honored and humbled to stand there, seemingly on the edge of the planet. But we had to admit, we were not home, even if we didn't yet know why.

As we walked from the beach back to our tent, Amy wondered aloud if we should finish the Idaho cabin. In college we'd spent a couple of summer vacations on the ranch together, working until we had a little log structure shelled in and roofed, which is how we'd left it for several years. She brought it up in an offhand way at first—"maybe . . ."—but as we walked and she spoke, the idea began to take on momentum for her. We could own our dream, our outpost in the woods, she reasoned, not rent somebody else's. We could start our settled lives, our so-called adult lives, with something solid and truly ours.

Much as I felt a flood of optimism and rightness filling my mind with the thought, I mostly listened, a change for us. In the course of our lives together Amy has listened to and adopted so many of my dreams, and building the cabin had been in my heart since I was a child. Could she share that? I finally asked her that evening as we sat at the picnic table at our campsite. Could it be as much hers as mine?

"I've got some ideas too," she said and went into the tent for her journal. When she returned she tore out a blank sheet and sketched a simple floor plan—a little sunken living room with a writing desk for me and a woodstove, both in front of a big picture window; across the room and facing the stove and window, a couch where we could curl up and watch the fire and the moonrise over the mountain at the same time. She sketched a tiny kitchen in the back with a half-loft above. When she was finished with the layout, she drew Yukon, curled into a shaggy semicircle on the floor in front of the couch.

We left the next morning. We turned that windshield-chipped, sagging truck around, toward this ground my family has lived on for more than forty years. And now we've been here five months, and the cabin is at last habitable. Barely.

My family's place is three miles from the tiny, general-store-post-office-tavern-cemetery settlement of Westmond, and twelve miles south of the county seat of Sandpoint, a glorious little mountain town on a lake. There's even a small city beach for Amy to walk. I grew up visiting summers and Christmases, and though I've never lived here for more than a couple months at a time, it is as close to home as any place I've ever known.

Originally, my dream had been wilderness without compromise, a place still as open and pure as our imaginations, somewhere where grizzlies wander endless territories. I wanted Alaska. But I wanted a home too, a place that would belong to Amy and me and to which we could belong. Idaho is threatened. The buzz of more and more cars and chainsaws drives the last of the grizzlies into the high country. But Idaho is still stunning, big and wild enough to make us aware of our existence every day we're here, to keep us from the complacency of unnoticed years that quietly robs so many people of whom they might have become. And if we can last through this pregnancy, and if Amy still wants to stay once the baby arrives, Idaho can be ours. Like the few remaining grizzlies, we'll hole up

7

in these mountains, in what's left of the unspoiled country, and raise our young.

Amy's been having sharp pains in her abdomen several times a day, and when we went to bed last night we resolved to call the doctor in the morning.

We got up early. The fire had burned down to a smolder, and I could see my breath as I got dressed. We didn't bother to stoke the stove or add more wood, or even make up the bed. Instead, we climbed into the truck and drove our winding, half-mile road down to my uncle Steve's house to use the phone.

First, Amy talked with the nurse; then the nurse put the doctor on. Amy began to answer more and more specific questions—"Yes, stabbing, sudden pain then dull ache. No, to one side. When I cough. For a few days, well, also before I found out. No. No."

I stood in the kitchen buttering toast, listening to her out in the dining room. I'd been awake half the night up in the cabin loft, where we'd moved our bed. On the verge of sleep, I'd kept seeing the sentence in our pregnancy book that ends ". . . abdominal pain can be a symptom of ectopic pregnancy." According to the book an ectopic pregnancy can be deadly and the only cure is surgery, a surgical abortion really. When I walked into the dining room, the long table was empty except for Amy. My uncle's family was gone—at school, out with the cows, on their way to work.

The quiet around us was eerie. Meals at that table are usually a chaos of conversation, laughter, smells, tastes, and trips to the kitchen. Though members of my family still stop by to visit my grandparents in the old farmhouse every day or two, my uncle Steve and aunt Marguerite's big log home has become the center of activity on the ranch in the last dozen years. It's the gathering place for our family feeds. Along with Steve and Marguerite, their two youngest children—Jeremiah and Jennifer (a teenager and a ten-year-old)—and the occasional spare Johnson visiting for a weekend, Amy and I lived there throughout the fall while we worked on the cabin. And though we're glad now to be in our own snug, quiet little place up on the hill, we often wander down the twisty road through the woods for more of those chaotic meals.

But that morning, sitting at the head of the table describing her pains to the doctor, Amy looked so alone. She's a small woman and the room around her was cavernous and I felt far away, helpless with my cooling toast and butter knife. The doctor wanted to see us that day.

I've been thinking of this pregnancy as ours, but at the Sandpoint Women's Health Clinic, when Amy went in to see the doctor, she went in by herself. So I sat there in the waiting room, waiting. In the chairs opposite me, two young girls with rounded bellies protruding from their unzipped jackets were talking about their baby showers. One's was coming up; the other had just had hers. She knew her baby was a boy so had asked for and received cowboy things—a mobile, a little quilt with hats and boots on it, stuffed horses, tiny Wranglers with elastic waists and snap-up inseams. Her sister and her sister's husband were renovating their garage attic into an apartment for her and Kyle. Whether Kyle was the dad or the baby, I didn't catch.

After a while I picked up a magazine and thumbed distractedly through it until I came to an article on a training camp for environmental activists over in Montana. The young people in the pictures going through ropes courses and sitting cross-legged on the ground talking looked a lot like Amy and me, same loose clothes, same hiking boots and unkempt hair. They were learning to use sound bites and lobby politicians,

9

according to the article, and to use "The System" to save the forest. Some of them said they were put off by being told to dress differently and act and talk like they were part of a system they did not respect, a system they thought was responsible for screwing up the planet. The camp leaders were older, experienced. They'd chosen haircuts as an evil lesser than clear-cuts.

Idealism and adulthood. I supposed the camp leaders were right. Or at least more effective in their approach. Still, sitting there in the doctor's waiting room, I felt for the young environmentalists. They didn't want to grow up, didn't want to decide between their free, rebellious, often whimsical forms of self-expression (their tie-dyed shirts, beards, bare feet, and nose rings) and the forests they loved so sincerely.

Two and a half years ago Amy and I were married among a stand of old growth birch on a cliff top above Lake Superior. No one was in bare feet or tie-dye, but there were plenty of beards and ponytails and Amy wore a dress and hat her grandmother had sewn out of silk dappled with color—mostly purple. Her little cousin T.J. emerged from the trees and walked down the aisle carrying a bowlful of lake water with our rings submerged in it.

In the vows she'd written, Amy compared our love to those northern Michigan woods in which she'd felt safe and peaceful since she'd been a child. The young preacher blessed the congregation with sage smoke fanned by an owl feather. Then, when the rings were on our fingers and the ceremony was almost at its end, he lifted the bowl of lake water from the little, makeshift altar. "Who wants this?" he asked with a mischievous grin and, without waiting for a reply, tossed the water in an arch over all our heads. Laughter, then bright guitar music and singing rose in the June sunshine.

Now, in the days since the pregnancy test showed a pink

line, we've been poring over *What to Expect When You're Expecting*. It already seems like a previous life, the days we didn't worry about ectopic pregnancy and insurance coverage and whether or not the cabin will be warm enough next winter for a baby. We used to talk about biking New Zealand's South Island and about how I could delay finding a job long enough to finish a book of poems. Now, we want desperately to be given the responsibility.

I finished the magazine article and guessed that by then Amy and the doctor would be talking. The awkward, unpleasant examination would be over, so I figured I'd go on back and join them. When I walked into the corridor, they were already chatting outside the exam room. Their voices and postures were casual. Dr. Bowden was a young woman in a sack dress, long johns, and hiking boots—a cross between the activists in the article and their elder instructors, I thought. Also, with her blond, pageboy haircut and round, kind face, she looked a little like Maria in *The Sound of Music*.

Amy said something and Dr. Bowden chuckled. She handed Amy a little paper wheel with numbers printed on it, a round calendar with the weeks of gestation, I saw when I got closer. "Everything's fine," Amy said, and the doctor smiled her agreement. I thought of Maria's smile when the children run to her room during the thunderstorm.

"I'm nine weeks," Amy said.

"Due July 18th," Bowden added.

The pain had been normal, just ligaments stretching and adjusting as the baby began to grow.

As we walked out the double doors and into the early night, I told Amy that the Sandpoint Women's Health Clinic had been a Safeway grocery store when I was a kid.

"My uncle Richard worked here. I remember picking him up with my dad."

The building looked completely new now, new covered entry and new brick steps leading out toward the parking lot.

"I'll have a lot to tell our baby about this place."

"I'm glad you're going to get that chance," Amy said.

Our truck was alone at the end of the snow-filled lot, and as we walked toward it we could see the Cabinet Mountain Range under a full moon. I unlocked Amy's door but we didn't get in. Instead we stood there awhile, arms around each other, the keys warm in my hand.

As I was driving the long bridge across Lake Pend Oreille into Sandpoint one afternoon, a bald eagle, the first I've seen in northern Idaho in at least ten years, crossed not twenty feet above my windshield. A bolt of electricity shot through my chest, as though I were suddenly plugged in, brought to life myself, and I banged the wheel with both palms and shouted, "yes!" I said it suddenly, ecstatically, without thinking, without asking myself, "yes what?"

The other night Amy and I talked economics, adding up the numbers out loud in bed, staring at the exposed insulation in the loft ceiling just above us. We've spent down the small savings we took with us to Alaska and racked up thousands more dollars in debt on sinker nails and mortar and cinder blocks and metal roofing and top-grade pine for the heavy, iron-bolted front door. We can't afford to punch in a well so we pack water. We've had to hire a big front-end loader to clear all the snow that's been falling. The plow bill for the ranch in November was over four hundred dollars, two hundred of that our share for the cabin road. If we weren't building on my grandparents' land, we couldn't afford to build at all. I have a writing grant that will keep small checks coming every two weeks through April. I don't know what will happen then, but for now I build on the cabin, write, and work on the ranch.

"Do you ever plan to use your degree?" Amy asked.

"I don't know," I said. In the five months since we've been in Idaho, I've been hedging on my long-term plan to teach college writing.

"That's frightening for me," she said.

"Me too," I sighed.

And I am frightened. Throwing hay to the cows in the snowed-over meadow or driving the county road where it crosses Westmond Creek and the woods open up and the mountains suddenly rise from the trees all around me, I'm often struck with fear. So much in our lives—years of college and the accompanying student loan debt, our passions for art, for good movies and healthy food and young friends— points toward our not staying here very long. Sometimes, our big decisions already seem made, and these days in the woods seem only a detour from an inevitable life elsewhere.

"So why did you get it? The degree?" She had an impatient, tired edge to her voice. "I mean, if you're never going to teach?"

"I didn't say I wasn't ever going to teach."

"Well, we're not getting by like this. Not in any long-term way. This can't go on forever or we'll go bankrupt."

"Great. Wonderful. Then let's give up," I said, and suddenly we were just another young couple bickering about money in America.

"Did I say I want to give up? You're not listening to me."

"What do you want, then?"

"Forget it," she said.

"Oh sure, I'll just forget it," I snapped. But she'd been right.

I hadn't been listening, and if I didn't turn the conversation around I'd miss whatever she wanted to tell me.

"I'm sorry," I said. "I'm scared, too."

"I don't want to leave here," Amy answered. "It's just hard not having a long-term plan."

"I'll look for something in the spring when the grant is up. I just don't know what the hell it'll be in northern Idaho."

"I found my job," she said, not unkindly.

Her job. I knew that was a big part of her frustration and fear. For two months she's been working at a small psychiatric hospital down in Coeur d'Alene, almost an hour drive south of the cabin, down a windy, forest-lined road, but she will likely be laid off in the next month or two. She was the last hired, and the hospital is running low on psychiatric patients—everyone in northern Idaho must be nursing their wounded brains and hearts deep in the woods, rather than coming to town for mental health care.

If we didn't need the money, Amy wouldn't care about the threat of a layoff. It's not a job she likes, calling insurance companies all day, trying to twist their arms into giving the patients in her unit another week or two of desperately needed treatment. It's not the job she went to graduate school for, not nearly the job she left behind in Michigan where she did social work at a public agency for people with no insurance. The Coeur d'Alene hospital job buys some of the building supplies and makes the student loan payments. It keeps this dream going, but that's about the only satisfaction it gives Amy.

"So what *do* you want?" I asked.

"I want to stay home with the baby. That's all."

"Of course you do," I said quietly. Of course. Of course she wants to be the first voice, the first presence in the room when our child wakes up. Of course work, especially her current work, seems trivial to her compared with walking in the woods with our baby on her back, sun filtering down through dense pine. And of course I want that freedom for her.

Then, like snow falling all at once from an overloaded fir—pounds of snow tumbling from every branch and landing with a crushing thud—reality came down on me. Here I am, I realized, broke, unemployed, a husband about to be a father in a cabin months and many dollars away from being done. The cold worms its way through unsealed gaps where the log walls meet the framing at the doors and gables and windows ... and the windows—still just sheets of plastic and, when it's especially cold, tacked-up blankets for curtains. We hang our mugs and dish towels on nails driven into bare studs in the kitchen. We haven't even begun to plumb and don't have a dime saved to get running water in the spring anyway. And, because Amy was pregnant before she took the psychiatric hospital job (though we didn't yet know), her health insurance won't pay for her prenatal care and the delivery even if she keeps the job or we somehow manage to pay the premiums ourselves to continue the insurance. At that moment we weren't romantics following our passion for the wilderness up into a mountain cabin; we were a couple irresponsible adolescents. Or, more accurately, I was. Amy has a job.

"Maybe I'll buy a lottery ticket at Westmond Store tomorrow," she said.

"Don't say that. That's what desperate people say. We'll be okay. If we can't make this work, college teaching would be good for a while, I suppose. While you stayed home with the baby." I could imagine meeting Amy and our child between classes on the campus lawn of some small state university.

"I only want to for a little while, just at first," she said.

"I know. I'm not going to complain if it comes to that. We've at least got options. Dennis, now he has reason to complain."

My cousin Dennis, my uncle Steve's oldest son, grew up on

the ranch and drives a forklift at the sawmill north of Sandpoint. He works five ten-hour, all-night shifts a week, driving home after each shift to his wife and baby at dawn, crawling in bed to rest his sore, twenty-one-year-old body beside his family for an hour or two before the sun, or his baby's crying, or a knock on the door starts his day all over again. We've never talked about what he imagines, if he still has some vision of how his existence might be, or if he already thinks the time for new beginnings is forever behind him.

"He's offered to get me on at the mill," I said.

"I wouldn't want you to do that. Let's just play it by ear." Amy rolled over on her side. "We don't have to have all the answers tonight."

But I wanted the answers. I wanted right then to know how to have it all. I wanted to be a provider. But having found our way here, I wanted to stay and raise our child in this cabin on this land. Having a family, having children, is the most natural thing I can imagine doing in this life. In the sense that parenthood is biological, that it unfolds naturally out of love, it even seems easy. I'm beginning to suspect, though, that it might also be the hardest thing anyone ever does, the thing that most deeply alters who you are and what you want and sends you furthest into the unknown territory beyond yourself. The true wilderness.

As our quiet and the night closed around our bed, I was already thinking about how, if we did eventually leave Idaho and this dream, our summer visits back here would end. I was thinking about how I would mourn as we packed up the truck and bolted the door behind us for another year. How I would remember when we lived here all the time and wonder, as we drove down the road toward the highway, if maybe there had been something I missed, some way to keep the place and life I loved while doing what I must to become the father this baby deserves.

A fire burned in the stove as Amy dug through a box of tissue-wrapped ornaments to hang on our fresh-cut Christmas tree. She's been having a tough time. In addition to wondering how we'll get by once the baby is born, she's been homesick. She's crazy about Christmas, and this will be the first one she's spent away from her family in upper Michigan. Every year she and her sister and parents have picked out a tree under the string of light bulbs in the parking lot at Meister's Greenhouse and Nursery in Marquette, driven home with the chosen tree tied to the roof, and stayed up late listening to carols on the radio and decorating the boughs with many of the same ornaments that she was now unpacking here, 1,700 miles away, while humming "Jingle Bells."

"This one is my dad's," she said as she hung a tiny pair of snowshoes on a low bough. It occurred to me that her child-like Christmas spirit in the face of her loneliness for home was just one more instance of Amy's characteristic pragmatism getting her through change, one more example of the emotional grace and optimism that I've admired and tried to learn from since we first met in high school.

Our tree looks nothing like the bushy, perfectly symmetrical, cone-shaped ones her family buys from that suburban parking lot. It's a little white fir, and you can see right through it to the log wall on the other side. One evening earlier in the week, Amy and I skied the ranch looking for a tree, and she spotted this one at the far end of the alfalfa field.

"That's it. That's the one," she said. She skied up behind me, pulled a handsaw and rope out of my pack, and crawled in under the lowest boughs not buried in snow to cut the trunk.

When she'd fallen the little tree, Amy tied one end of the rope around the trunk a few branches up from the fresh cut, which was already filling the still, cold air with the smell of sap. I gave her my pack and tied a loop in the other end of the rope and slung it over my shoulder, and we skied home in the dusk—a tall, broad-chested, bearded man and a small, athletic woman—the tree sliding along behind us.

While she hung family ornaments, I hung a string of battery-powered Christmas lights that I'd bought weeks before to surprise her. When we were done we stood arm in arm at the opposite end of the cabin looking at our masterpiece. The battery-powered lights glowed amid little plastic penguins and Santas and snowmen. We've been married through three Christmases now, but this was our first tree.

"I want to get some film soon," Amy said, "so we can take a picture and send it to my mom and dad."

"It's a little thinner inside than it looked out in the field."

"It's perfect. Very woodsy." She considered it a moment more. "Authentic."

"Authentic is right," I agreed.

"Sometimes authentic is harder," she said, a sudden, sad catch in her voice.

"We'll take our baby back to Michigan for Christmases," I said.

"But I wouldn't want our baby to miss this. I love this. Maybe we can have a tree here too every year. Cut it down and decorate it before we go."

"Sure."

"It's not that I don't want to be here. I really do."

"I know, but it's good to hear you say it."

In the morning, we hiked down to Steve and Marguerite's and

found Steve out in the barnyard, harnessing Princess, the black mare, for the sleigh.

"How'd the tree turn out?" he asked without looking up as he cinched the bellyband on Princess's harness. "I was skiing the alfalfa field and saw the stump and the track where you dragged it away." Steve's been keeping an eye on us, I think, looking for signs that we'll be staying.

"Good," Amy said, grabbing a fistful of oats for Princess from the grain box. She opened her hand and the horses' lips slid around on her palm, clapping up the feed. "You guys will have to come up later for egg nog and see it."

When Steve finished with Princess he led her to where the sleigh was parked under a lean-to, hitched her up, then went in the house and got Marguerite, my ten-year-old cousin Jennifer, and an armload of blankets.

The five of us piled into the little sleigh and wrapped ourselves in the blankets and Steve gave a click. We slid out of the lean-to and onto the driveway. Steve and Marguerite are in their forties, a generation older than Amy and me. While Steve's cottony blond hair and boyish smile look just as they do in pictures from twenty years ago, his chest has broadened from the years of work and Marguerite's flowing black hair is streaked with gray she doesn't pretend away with dye. They look like the farm people they are, people Amy and I could, if we are lucky and strong enough, become a lot like.

As we passed my grandparents' house, Marguerite said, "Let's stop on the way back. They'll want to come out and see us."

We rode down past the mailboxes at the end of our ranch drive and out onto the county road, singing Christmas carols to the jingle of actual sleigh bells. As we went by a neighbor's place, Amy said, "Think how we'd look if someone peeked out their window."

"Like a Christmas card," Jennifer said.

Authentic *is* harder. Amy's right. The life we want costs; in homesickness and frustration and economic angst, it costs. But it's a good life. I've spent Christmas on Greyhound buses and in airports, in apartments in cities where it never snows, and in houses in far northern Michigan where it snows sometimes for six months. One Christmas I spent in a car driving south through Oklahoma on my way to Central America. But now, writing this in our kitchen by candlelight, soft Christmas music on the radio, Amy in the loft sleeping the deep, steady sleep of a future mother, it seems to me that, even though I don't have a damn clue how we're going to keep this life going, or even if we will at all, this is as content as I've ever been.

One June morning when I was nine or ten years old, I woke panicked. *Are they gone? Don't let them be gone yet,* snapped in my drowsy brain like the sudden crackle of skillet grease from downstairs.

Up in the low bedroom of my grandparents' farmhouse the hazy blue light of an overcast, wet dawn was already pushing its way in through the gauzy curtains that always hung closed in front of the one small, gable-end window, framed by more curtains—floral yellow, plastic ones that were never closed. I saw that my sister and parents were still in their beds. It couldn't be that late if my dad was still asleep. But at least in the myth I made of them in my mind my uncles were often out feeding the cattle or up in the woods in the cold dark with only the dimmest hint of light behind the stars above the mountain.

It was summer vacation, my first morning to wake up in Idaho after an entire school year of dreaming, of every few days taking the plane tickets from the refrigerator butter tray, where my parents kept them, and staring at our seat assignments typed onto that stiff, thick paper along with the date and departure and arrival times and the destination. Spokane. Where my uncle Lester would pick us up for the drive across the state line and into the mountains. And here I was, *finally*, and they might already be out somewhere without me.

All three of my uncles were schoolteachers. It was summer vacation for them too, and they'd want to make the most of every day of it, I thought, finding my jeans and flannel shirt where I'd left them on the floor. I'd known I'd wear that flannel shirt in Idaho. It had hung in my closet all fall, waiting beside the *Star Wars* and *Keep on Truckin'* T-shirts. That shirt looked like the shirts my uncles wore. It looked like work, like the shirt of a serious ranch kid. I never wore it to my suburban school, of course, but it was my most prized article of clothing.

From the smell and sound of grease, breakfast was still on the stove, and I could hear hushed voices as I came down the narrow, steep stairs.

"Morning, Jon!" my uncle Richard announced from his chair at the table in long, drawn-out syllables of surprise, exclamation, and delight that were, nonetheless, somehow still a whisper. He stood and with the big, lanky, exaggerated, put-'er-there gesture of a marionette shook my hand. "How'd you sleep, Partner?"

My uncle Steve winked.

"Coffee, Son?" my grandfather offered, lifting the thermos from his end of the long table. It was the first time he or anyone had offered me coffee.

I nodded. I told them all, Richard and Lester and Steve and my grandparents, that I'd slept like a log. I was ready to get after it. Hadn't Lester said something on the way up late last night about getting into the woods to cut some standing dead for my grandparents' woodshed? It wouldn't surprise me now if one of them told me I'd still been in sock feet.

But we ate first. Eggs and hash browns and bacon and sausage. (The smell and sizzle of meat brings back such memories of those mornings I wonder still how I ever gave it up.) My grandmother worked the new electric range and the old, black and chrome, wood-burning Monarch simultaneously to fix it all. And if I *was* in sock feet someone would have dug out a pair of one of my uncle's old work boots—leather stiff almost to petrifaction and a size or so too big—from behind the kindling box. I wore one or another pair like them every time I was on the farm, and when they rubbed and hurt I never said a thing until my feet blistered and I had to revert back to my stupid sneakers for a couple days.

Through breakfast I split my attention between the conversation, which would have been about our flight into Spokane or everyone's school years or—if my grandmother was feeling fired up about the "damn, fat cat capitalists," as she often was—politics, and the room. I took inventory—the long buffet tilting slightly with the floor, my grandfather's collection of plastic horses and covered wagons atop the kitchen cabinets, his guitar hanging on the wall, the stovepipe curving over into the whitewashed block chimney, the little wire glove-drying rack beside stacked high with fuzzy yellow, Handy Andy chore gloves. The picture my grandmother painted of a waterfall in an oak and maple forest in autumn. My grandfather's age-speckled hand pouring blackstrap molasses from the bottle with the rabbit on the label into his cup of flaxseed tea. (He'd be offering me a taste of the concoction any time now, with a mock off-handed, "Jon, you care for a little of this here?" and my uncle Richard would cringe and shudder.) All of it was still here. All of it matched up with the details I car-

22

ried around with me every day, and so I must be who I believed I was, a part of this.

The house wasn't, and still isn't, particularly stately. It's not like the broad-shouldered, three-story farmhouses with wrap-around porches and multiple chimneys rising skyward that I've come to know along midwestern back roads. No, it's one story except for one low bedroom upstairs. Its white paint's perpetually flaking and fading to gray, but the forest green metal roof and mint green trim hold their colors. Early in the twentieth century, when the valley was all Humbird Lumber Company land, the house, or at least the core of it, had been a logging camp kitchen. It had been dragged on log skids from site to site until it ended up on the ridge it now occupies. And when the Humbird Lumber Company moved on from here, they sold it with the land to a family by the name of Hicks (hence, my whole life the label "hick" has carried with it a fair share of positive, if not unstereotypical, associations for me).

In addition to clearing pastureland and building the barn and machine shed, the Hicks built on to the house, and the original one-room building became what is still the big, open kitchen/front room. My grandparents bought the place from the Hicks when my dad, who is the oldest of the four boys, was in high school. Remembering that first morning of summer vacation now, the boy voices of my dad and his brothers, and the voices of the Hicks, and the voices of all those Humbird loggers long before them seemed almost audible, coming from somewhere in there as I rode in the pickup bed with Steve and Lester and their chainsaws away from the house and smoke trailing up from the chimney.

My grandparents pulled back the curtain and waved. My grandfather had said he'd stay behind until my parents and sister were up and fed. Then if the rain was still holding off, he'd walk with my dad out to find us.

My uncle Richard drove up the hill behind the barn and into the woods in low gear. The engine groaned a steady slow groan and the saws jostled around with the gas cans and axes and bark chips from countless previous loads of wood. I held on to the sides of the bed and ducked when we passed under low limbs. In addition to my flannel shirt and threadbare jeans and hand-me-down boots, I had on a pair of those yellow, Handy Andy gloves and one of the old-fashioned, wide-brimmed, metal logger's hats my grandfather kept in the woodshed.

Much as it held the things of this place in my mind between those childhood visits, memory has done its invisible work on the past. In my memory we drove up into the forest and back with load after high-stacked load of wood, and my cousins Eric and Robert were there at the house when we'd return, along with my dad and grandfather, and we all passed the stove-length logs to Richard as fast as we could as he frantically stacked them in the woodshed and periodically shouted, "More wood!" In my memory we had the woodshed crammed full by day's end.

But that was just as likely some other day, or series of days. Or maybe even some other summer. What matters though is that it was here. Living on my family's place now, I'm discovering that home is that locale in the mind and the world where, through all the changes in both, the two fit.

When I'm driving back from town or the Westmond Store and I reach the mailboxes at the end of the county road and look up at the hilltop house, the pasture sloping up to it and the woods behind, the scene looks the same. And who I am is still upstairs behind the little window, waking up.

Yesterday, on our ski through the alfalfa field, we found tracks, big round tracks of some heavy animal that had crossed onto our place from the north. The tracks were too deep to see any definition in the hoof prints, but they were accompanied by coyote tracks back in the brush. Some drama had been playing itself out in our woods. The round tracks were far bigger than deer tracks, and there was no evidence of a belly dragging in the deep snow that would accompany a loose cow's tracks.

"Could it be a horse?" Amy asked.

"Could have been, but in winter loose horses usually head toward the shrubs and hay of houses and barns, not deeper into the woods. Maybe a moose."

"A moose!" Amy was delighted. Moose are native to her own northern Michigan and are a kind of signature animal for those woods.

No one's seen a moose on our land before, but my aunt had seen one recently on the highway about five miles up the valley. There was no other obvious explanation.

As we skied farther out to the remotest part of the ranch, we saw that the little coyote tracks were gone, but we discovered more and more of the big tracks. Fresh. From the last few hours. Something, several somethings, it now looked like, had been walking the fence line looking for a place to cross over. Whatever it was could really jump. There was no hair caught in the barbed wire where the tracks finally did cross over into the steep, thick woods we call the Back Slope.

"This is a good sign," I said to Amy as we stared into the woods where the tracks disappeared. "I want so desperately for this corner of the world to stay wild."

"It seems pretty wild to me."

"That makes me so happy to hear."

We skied until dark, and then Amy returned to the cabin. I skied down to my uncle Steve's house, where I called the neighboring ranchers and asked permission to follow those tracks onto their properties in the morning. On the second call I reached a young woman whose mother owns the place to the southwest of ours. She told me the tracks were elk.

"Five cows," she said. "I saw them the other day when I was up there looking for a Christmas tree."

Stunned, I thanked her for the news, hung up, and skied through the dark back to the cabin, eager to tell Amy.

Elk! I imagined I might come upon one in the night, the silhouette of its huge head and shoulders just visible up the trail in the starlight filtering down through the forest canopy. The record snows must have driven them down off Butler Mountain and into this valley for the first time in my lifetime. In this migration they were returning to ground they'd given up long ago. I want to believe that they are bringing the wilderness down with them from the high country and giving it back to us. If they find it safe and the foraging good, they might keep coming back. Every day we somehow manage to pay our Visa bill and buy groceries and keep living in the cabin will be one more chance we might see them. And if they do keep coming back, and if we can last long enough, we can give our baby that same chance.

It's a Saturday morning, the Saturday before Christmas Day. The cabin smells like last night's woodsmoke and snow. The temperature outside has climbed to twenty-seven, so we're relatively warm even without windows. In fact, I've taken down the blankets we had hung for insulation over the front window holes, and daylight shines through the clear plastic.

Last night, I heard the shush as snow slid off our metal roof and the thumps where it landed, adding to the snowbank that was already almost all the way up to the eaves. It's a snug, lazy feeling, having all that snow around us. We're dug in, Amy and Yukon sleeping late up in the loft.

It occurs to me that our life is, I'm afraid to say perfect, but at least blessed. At least for now it is. Yesterday we skied the property line. Every couple hundred feet we stopped, and Amy dug a fistful of hay from my backpack and spread it on the snow. If they wander back onto the place, we won't make a habit of feeding them, but we want the elk to come here again and get comfortable passing through.

At night, when I pause from chopping wood in front of the cabin and look out over the valley, I can see no house lights or roads, just the moon and stars lighting the snow. I can't imagine the world in thirty or forty years, but I can imagine my daughter (always in my imagination she's a daughter) standing in the alfalfa field behind the cabin, watching elk cross in the ghostly glow of a full moon. In my vision it is spring, the field spongy between the last patches of snow, and the woman my daughter will be curls her cold, bare toes for joy, joy at the new wet grass, joy at the elk heading back up to their mountain, where there are still no lights.

As soon as we arrived in Idaho late last summer, Amy and I quit taking measures to prevent her from getting pregnant and began the most physically passionate season of our marriage so far. Every time we were together was charged with the knowledge that it could be the beginning of some new human being's story. Often we wandered out to the woods and fields as the aspen and tamarack turned, peppering the dark green slopes of Butler Mountain with autumn yellow above us, and we lingered a long time, the afternoon sun luxuriously warm on our skin or a fleece blanket wrapped around us against the cool, inky air of evening.

More than ten years ago, we were part of the same newly formed circle of friends, artsy kids from drama club, and she'd seen me walking home from the high school, pulled over, and offered me a ride. It was only four blocks, but I remember the quiver of electricity I felt being alone in her presence for the first time, her slight frame in those sun-faded overalls that were splattered with pink and yellow from the theater set we'd all been painting that day. Folded on the back seat of the Subaru wagon where I tossed my book bag was a knitted afghan I'd seen wrapped around the shoulders of Amy and her two best girlfriends at football games. I can still see its red and white and black diamond pattern as if looking at a photograph. Its presence made the car around us feel domestic and cozy. Which is how the space around us has felt ever since. It's the kind of space that makes you want to forget your cautions and calculations and give yourself over to its every possibility, the kind of space you can make a family in.

But through all the years since—a decade—we'd remained just the two of us. Then, last June we decided it was time to try to have a child. Both of us knew the exact day we decided. We knew exactly where we were and exactly what we were doing. And after that—the seventh day of our journey toward Alaska, in the Canadian settlement of White River in the Yukon Territory—the only question was how quickly we could settle on a destination and get off the road.

The day we decided it was time, we were driving. We were twenty-some miles north of White River, on an unpaved stretch of the AlCan Highway, when Amy spotted a bear cub.

"There. On the side of the road," she pointed, and I slowed the truck way down and aimed wide into the opposite lane.

"Stop!" she hollered as we passed. "Pull over. It's a little kid!"

And I saw it was—kneeling, curled over into a ball, arms up

over his or her head for protection, I realized, from the spray of gravel and dirt we'd have kicked up if we'd been speeding by as others must have.

I stopped the truck and we sat there, a hundred feet or so up the road. Amy rolled down her window, adjusted the passenger side mirror, and peered into it. "That's weird."

I looked down into my own mirror and saw the child standing up. He was a small boy, barely school age, in a dark, quilted jacket on a warm, sunny day.

"Could a school bus have let him off?" I asked, though I knew how absurd that was. We hadn't passed a single house or even a driveway in the half-hour since White River. This was easily the wildest stretch of road I'd ever been on.

"A school bus?"

"I don't know. Maybe the parents dropped him off. To scare him or something."

"We should go back."

"What if it was the parents? Some asshole dad trying to teach him a lesson? They'll come back."

"I don't care if they do." Amy was insistent. "We should at least see if he's okay."

I backed the truck up and parked, and when we got out we saw he was very much not okay. His face was dusty and streaked with dried tears. His lips were cracked, and his palms were wrapped sloppily in gauze. His fingers were swollen and covered with insect bites. He just stood there in front of us and stared at the ground. He had the straight, dark hair and dark skin of a Native American.

"Hi," Amy said, leaning down to try to catch his eye and telling him our names. "Do you live around here?"

The boy shook his head and kept his eyes down. Yukon leaned out of the truck window and whined. The boy glanced at him for just a moment.

29

I asked if someone dropped him off, and he shook his head again.

"What's your name, Sweetie?" Amy asked.

"Tom."

"How did you get here, Tom?"

"Walked."

"Where did you walk from?"

His eyes raised toward the mountains. "Up there," and as he pointed, the cuff of his coat pulled back slightly from the back of his wrist and I saw a black number nine.

"Are you alone?" I asked.

Tom lowered his arm and the nine disappeared back into the coat sleeve as he looked to the ground again.

Amy knelt in front of him. "Are your folks around?"

Nothing.

"Are they up there?" She nodded toward the mountains.

Nothing.

"Are you hungry, Kiddo?"

He nodded and his eyes went wet.

"We've got a couple Pop-Tarts in the truck," I said and trotted over to get them. When I came back I brought the dog, who wagged his tail and walked straight up to Tom, licked his face, and sat down.

As Tom shoved bite after bite of Pop-Tart into his mouth and stroked Yukon's head, I saw the nine on the boy's wrist was followed by other numbers. Three numbers and a dash, the beginning of a phone number in black felt marker on his skin.

I asked if he needed a telephone.

"My dad said to call my aunt."

"Is your dad around here? Did he drop you off?" Amy asked.

He shook his head.

"You're sure?"

"He said call my aunt. He left." Tom was crying again. He ate the last of the Pop-Tarts and pushed up his sleeve to show us. After the numbers were the words *please call!*

"We'd like to take you to a telephone and get you a meal," Amy said and put her hand on his shoulder.

He lowered his sleeve and resumed petting Yukon.

"Would that be okay?"

Tom nodded.

Yukon is a Great Pyrenees, which look something like a slightly taller, white version of a Newfoundland. Or, if you use your imagination just a little, a polar bear. With him and Amy and me sitting side by side on the bench seat, our little Dodge Dakota pickup is close quarters. With the three of us and Tom it was jammed. Tom sat in the middle with his feet turned sideways to avoid the four-wheel-drive shifter, and Yukon sat with his back half on Amy's lap, his front legs straight and front paws on the floor and his chin resting on the dash where Tom could just reach to pet his head.

"Can you tell us where you live?" Amy asked over the top of Yukon's shaggy back.

"Anchorage."

"That's sure a long ways away. How'd you get way out here?"

"My dad."

"Your dad?"

"He busted out of jail. We walked."

It was as if, when he got in the car, Tom had decided we were on his side. That, or he'd decided he had no good alternative but to trust us.

"You can take off your coat," I said, and when he did I saw the number and message was repeated higher up and on the inside of his wrist and twice on his other arm.

Amy asked him what he and his dad were doing way out here.

"Camping," Tom answered. "We were going to Seattle."

"That's a long way," Amy said admiringly. "So, what do you think you'll want to eat for lunch?"

"A cheeseburger," Tom said and looked up into Amy's face, meeting her eyes for the first time.

The settlement of White River consisted of a café/general store/road house/gas station with rental cabins beside it and a grass airstrip in back with a faded orange wind sock that sagged from a log pole. We'd stayed in one of the cabins the night before, after pulling in under the broad Arctic daylight of 11:00 at night. In the morning we'd eaten breakfast in the homey, low-roofed café and chatted with Holly, our chipper waitress, who wore an apron, a nose ring, and spiky hair and told us she was the owner's daughter.

"You're back," Holly said as Amy and Tom and I stepped into the café. "But who is this little guy?"

The seven or eight other customers in the place glanced up at us.

Amy introduced Tom, and the three of us sat down at the table by the window. Tom hung his coat carefully on the back of his chair, and Holly brought us waters and a fistful of crayons.

"We're going to need to use your phone in a couple minutes to make a phone call for Tom, if we could," Amy said.

"Sure. Of course. Do you know what you want?" Holly asked the boy and stole a glance at the writing on his arm.

He pointed to the cellophane-wrapped Rice Krispie and M&M bars on the counter beside the cash register.

"Great choice. I made those."

"And a cheeseburger with fries," Amy added. "But bring the

Rice Krispie bar first, please. What do you like on your burger, Tom?"

"Just catsup," he said.

Holly brought the treat, and when she was gone, Tom reached into the breast pocket of his shirt and produced a folded piece of cardboard, which he handed to Amy. It was a piece of a raisin bran box with handwriting on the back in the same black felt marker as the writing on Tom's arm.

As Tom ate his Rice Krispie treat, Amy read the note, then asked Tom if she could show me. He sipped his glass of water through the straw and shrugged.

The note read:

> To whoever finds my Boy. Please take care of him. His name is Tommy and he is 6. I am traveling with him and can no longer take care of him. I am very sick with AIDS. Don't look for me. You won't find me. I will be food for bears I guess anyway. His Aunts phone number is 907-255-3616. I took him because his mom drinks and her boyfriend hits him. Kathy. I am sorry for everything. Derrick can never be his real Daddy. Don't let him hit Tommy anymore. I only wanted us to be a family.

"I've got pictures too. Wanna see?" Tom said, reaching into his coat pocket. He handed me a short stack of Polaroids. Each had a caption in the same black marker on the white paper border around the image: *Tommy and his Daddy who loves him very much*, it said below one of the boy, maybe a year younger, on a couch, smiling and sitting in the crook of a man's arm. The man looked mid-twenties and had a beard and light skin. NAS-CAR it said on his cap. He wasn't smiling, but he sat straight, his bearded chin high and his arm snugly around Tom's shoulders. *Tommy and his family*, it said below one of the boy and man and a slender Native American woman beside a Christmas tree. The man's face held the same proud expression, and

33

the woman and boy were smiling. There were other photos, too: *Tommy's cat, Tommy and Daddy on three wheelers, Daddy's Big Fish.*

I handed them to Amy, who looked at them, then folded the note and handed it all back to Tom.

"Nice pictures," she said as he looked through them himself. "Your cat looks like my cat when I was little."

"His name is Dusty."

"Mine was Fuzz."

Tom returned the photos to his coat pocket and the note to his shirt pocket and went off to the bathroom.

"He's so beautiful," I sighed. "He just opened right up. Could that be a lie about the mom's boyfriend?"

"Absolutely it could. So could the stuff about AIDS. But it could be true. The dad probably walked down to the road with him, where he told him to wait for someone to stop."

"He was probably watching us then from somewhere." It gave me a shiver to say it.

"I'd think so. If he was my child . . ." She trailed off.

I asked if we should call the aunt now, and Amy said we had to call the police and let them take it from there.

But I found myself not wanting to give responsibility for Tommy over to someone else, though I'd been with him for less than an hour. I suggested we could take him to Anchorage ourselves if the police would let us. Amy could explain to the police that she's a social worker. We could see to it that the dad's allegations of abuse were investigated. Maybe Tom could stay with us for a while. Until it got sorted out.

My lack of hesitation or ambivalence about taking care of him surprised me.

"Would they use us as foster parents, maybe? I mean, if he were removed from the house?"

Amy studied me and the corner of her mouth rose just a tiny bit.

"Buddy," she reached across the table and took my hand in hers. "He's got a mother. She's probably out of her mind right now. We have no idea what's going on at his house. He's been uprooted and traveled God knows how for hundreds and hundreds of miles. We'll tell the police to be certain, *certain*, the social worker in Alaska sees the note about the abuse. But he'll likely be going back there. The note will start a file on the family if there isn't one already. And it should mean someone will be keeping close tabs, checking to be sure he's safe. But even if they pull him, he'll probably end up with the aunt if she's familiar to him and can provide a good, stable home."

The bathroom door across the café opened and Tom headed toward us.

Amy leaned in even closer toward me and whispered quickly, "But you'd really want to take him in? If we could?"

"We don't even have a place to take him in to, but yeah. I think so. Yes."

"I love you so much," she said and kissed my cheek.

When Tom sat down, Amy unwrapped the bandages from his hands, which were puffy, red, and mapped with bites. She sent me out to her backpack in the truck for hand wipes and calamine lotion, got the dirt cleaned off, then smeared in the pink salve, working it gently between each finger, rubbing Tom's hands between hers.

"Is that some better, Kiddo?"

He nodded.

"You want to color?" Amy asked and turned over his place mat. "Just let me give you a quick buffing first."

Tom closed his eyes and scrunched up his face as Amy rubbed a hand wipe on his forehead and cheeks. She used another wipe for his chin then dabbed it on his nose. "There!

35

Now I'll color, too." She turned her own place mat over. "And while we color, Jonathan's going to call some people who can help us figure out how to get you home. Is that okay?"

"I guess so," he said absently as he picked up a crayon.

We waited half the day for the Royal Canadian Mounted Police to get there. Tom ate his burger. Then, a half-hour later, a grilled cheese sandwich and a chocolate chip cookie. Amy didn't press him for more information about his home or his trip or his dad, and I followed her lead. He'd get an interrogation soon enough, I supposed. Instead, he and Amy went on coloring and I joined them. Holly kept bringing us fresh place mats, on the backs of which Tom drew his house and his cat. He drew a picture of Yukon and one of our blue pickup. Amy drew penguins and furry little characters in sneakers. I drew mountains and clouds and trees.

Later, I taught Tom tic-tac-toe and explained to him that it's best to go first if you can and put your X in one of the corners. Holly brought out some cards and we invited her to join us as Amy taught us all to play go fish. Tom grew livelier. He smiled and even laughed a couple times.

It was as though we'd come into another world, another life, in which only marvelous things in bright crayon colors would happen. For a while it was.

But eventually the officer arrived, just as I'd known he would. His white crew-cab pickup pulled up outside, RCMP printed on the door and a rack of red lights across the roof.

"Look!" Amy said with an enthusiasm in her voice I recognized as feigned. "This is the guy who is coming to help us out, to help you out, Kiddo." She rolled up all of our drawings then took Tom's coat off the back of his chair and folded it over her arm. "Let's go meet him."

Amy and Tom and I went outside, and the officer smiled and extended his hand, first to Tom.

"I'm Andy," he said. He was tall, at least six inches taller than my six feet, and he had a Mountie hat complete with chin strap.

"Hi," Tom said nonchalantly and shook Andy's with his own little, bug-bit hand.

"What's your name?"

"Tom."

"Well, good to meet you, Tom." The officer turned to Amy and me and shook our hands. "Hi guys, Andy Greenspan."

When I went to say my name I found that my throat was tight and I had to work to keep a quiver from coming through my voice. I saw Amy's eyes were red.

Andy took down our names and the story in a notepad. Once we got started, Tom told most of it himself, proudly volunteering the note from his dad and the Polaroid photos.

"Well, Tom," Andy said, folding closed his notebook. "Can I interest you in a ride in my very awesome truck?"

"Sure."

"If you want to sit up in it for just a minute, we'll go. I'll just talk real quick with Jonathan and Amy." He helped the boy up into the cab.

"Here's his jacket," Amy said. "And some pictures we all drew." She handed them to Andy, who set them in the back seat.

Tom's eyes wandered over the complexities of the dashboard.

"You can make the lights go. Watch the reflection," Andy said. He pointed toward the café window then reached in and pushed a button. Then he pushed it off again.

Tom pushed the button and smiled at the pulsing lights winking back at him in the glass.

"We'll be right back," Andy said, and we stepped a few feet away from the truck.

37

"Thanks, you guys. You're good people. We've had cars stolen every few days then abandoned further down the road. I don't know if it's related, but I'm sure glad this little one isn't out in the bush anymore."

"Do you think you'll find the dad?" I asked.

"Out here?" He looked up the road. It disappeared into the wide valley and hundreds of thousands of uninhabited square miles. "Well, if someone doesn't want to get found, they don't."

If he was dying of AIDS, I hoped they didn't find him, that no matter what his crimes, he'd be allowed the dignity of his chosen death.

"Can we ask a favor?" Amy said.

"Sure."

"Can we give you a phone number and if the case workers in Alaska need someone to watch him for a little while they can call us?"

"Of course." He reached in his shirt pocket, took his notebook and pen back out, and wrote down the number.

"It's my parents' place, but they'll know how to get a hold of us. Also, be sure to pass the word that the social services agency in Anchorage needs to investigate the abuse allegation. They will anyway, but if you could communicate that message ahead with him."

We stepped back to Andy's truck with him and told Tom good-bye. He pulled his focus from the dash just long enough to look up and say, "Bye."

We stood and watched them drive off and Amy raised her hand to her mouth. "Oh, Bud," she sobbed.

"I know."

Of course, no one ever called us to take care of Tom. Amy knew they wouldn't, and she told me so again when we were back on the road that afternoon. But we couldn't let go of the thought of him. We talked on and on about him as we neared the Alaska line. Could he be so quick to trust as he was, not just of us but of Andy as well, and be living in an abusive home? Where would he be spending that night? He was so wonderful. Such a wonderful little boy.

That evening, beside our campfire, somewhere in the middle of a wilderness that opened beyond us to the northern end of the planet, I said to Amy, "I want to have kids."

She told me she knew that and said she wanted kids too, had wanted them since she was ten.

"I know, but I mean now. Soon anyway."

"Really?" She paused. "You really think you want to?"

"Being with that boy today was very good. I felt purposeful."

She told me that having kids isn't about what you need. It's about what they need.

"That's just it," I said and stirred the fire with a stick. "What I needed was to give him what he needed."

"That's good," she said in the wise, approving voice a spiritual teacher might use with a pupil who suddenly understands. "That's right."

Hours later, we were in our sleeping bags and every so often the slightest breeze riffled the roof of our tent above us.

"Buddy?" Amy said.

"I thought you were asleep."

"Nope. Just thinking. I hope Tom is sleeping."

"I bet he is. It's his first night in a bed in a long time."

"Yeah." She was quiet for a while. Then, "Buddy?"

"Yes?"

"I think it's time too."

Christmas morning I woke to the sounds of Amy's morning sickness as she vomited outside, followed by a long groan and deep sigh. I jumped up and poured a tall glass of 7 UP and brought it out to where she was standing holding her stomach.

"I'm okay," she said quietly and smiled a slight smile.

We stood out there in the crisp, blue morning and embraced for a few seconds. It was much colder than it had been recently, below zero I guessed. Wind moved across the mountain and through the valley, blowing plumes of spindrift up off the trees. They looked like little fires flaring up, fires of snow-dust flaring in the sunshine and burning out, dissolving into cold, bright air.

Next Christmas we will have a five-month-old.

Weekday mornings, when I do the farm chores, I feed the cattle in the open pasture downhill from the old farmhouse. The cattle follow me single file as I pull a purple plastic sled loaded with the first bale down the icy path. I spread the hay on the snow and the cattle eat, strands of hay hanging from either side of their mouths as they chew and watch me pull the empty sled back toward the barn for more bales.

I wouldn't have to feed hundreds of yards from the barn, even though that's where Steve does it when he feeds, but I do so, we both do so, for my grandfather. Where we feed, he can look out the kitchen window above the old, white enamel sink, where he does the morning dishes, shaves and splashes on his Aqua Velva, and he can see the small herd on his place.

My grandfather sold his cows when I was still a boy. After years of watching cattle prices fall and hay prices rise, he gave up his lifelong dream of being a rancher as he watched cow after cow loaded up a ramp into a big stock-trailer semi.

After a decade with only lazy dogs and barn cats on the place, my uncle bought a couple white-face Herefords and began to build up the modest herd here now. Counting the occasional pig and the sheep, there are only about thirty big animals here at once, forty or fifty in the spring, when the majority of the calves and lambs are born. They still don't pay for themselves most years. Most years the winter feed must be bought with my aunt and uncle's paychecks from teaching at the local public school. Financially at least, the animals make no sense. But here they are.

When my grandfather looked out his window and saw me feeding this morning, he came to the back porch, gave me a big, reaching wave with one hand, and cupped the other to his mouth to holler, "They look good, Son. Looking good." For a while, as long as hay prices don't go too high and Bonner County School District keeps writing paychecks, my grandfather *is* the head of a ranch, a cattleman in the mountains looking down on his herd, their breath rising in clouds that dissolve into the cold, dry, late December air.

Perhaps this land is the place for generations of outlandish ambitions. Maybe the cows, sheep, pigs, and horses are, like our cabin, just small parts of a larger collective vision, and what we're really raising here is hope. Five dark mornings a week Amy drives down our road toward the highway and the hospital and her windowless office. I watch her taillights until they disappear into the trees. I damp the fire, step into my heavy, quilted, manure-stinking coveralls, and zip them up.

Amy has been offered a dream job as the founding director of Sandpoint's first domestic violence shelter. When I woke up this morning and looked over at her, she was wide awake already. She had been for hours, she said, her brain jumping with excitement. She may still want to quit working when the baby is born, she told me, but for now she wants to do this.

We drove to town together. I'm a big believer in moral support, and I love to sit in coffee shops and write or read while I wait for Amy when she has an important interview or appointment. This morning she was going in to accept the job in person.

"I'm glad you won't be driving all the way down to Coeur d'Alene anymore," I said as we pulled onto the highway from the gravel county road, turning right, north, toward Sandpoint. The highway gets dangerous the further south you go. Halfway to Coeur d'Alene it twists through a long downgrade known as the Granite Hill. In the winter you can see the rubber smears and paint on crumpled guardrails, and where there are no guardrails, gouges in the snow along the shoulder like wounds, sometimes torn all the way open to the grass and dirt where cars have slid off the road. Logging trucks roar down out of the mountains, a flurry of sawdust and flakes of bark swirling behind their cribs stacked high and rocking with logs for the huge Louisiana Pacific Mill in Chilco. In the opposite lane, little cars zip north like bullets, headed toward the ski slopes.

But for all the comfort I took in knowing she wouldn't have to brave that long drive, I was still worried. Domestic violence work can be dangerous, and everywhere Amy goes our baby goes.

"Are you nervous at all?" I asked. "I mean about the abusers showing up there some night?"

"Not any more than I used to be at the Harbor House." The Harbor House was the women's shelter in Marquette. Right out of high school, Amy had taken her first job there and she'd stayed on all through her undergraduate college years.

Those were also the years when we were newly in love, our

young blood coursing with energy and conviction and affection for each other. One night she called me, her voice a rushed whisper, and she asked, "How do you put a distributor cap back on a motor?" She was with a woman from the shelter, a "client" in social work lingo. They were at this woman's house way out in the woods while her husband, who had a record of multiple arrests for assault, was away at work. When his wife had left one night in a police cruiser to seek refuge at the Harbor House, he'd pulled the distributor cap from her car so she couldn't come back and get it. Amy had driven the woman by the auto parts store, where they'd bought a replacement and, she informed me, the two of them were now outside, with the hood of the woman's car up, talking with me on a cell phone and thumbing through one of the husband's old mechanic's manuals.

But it isn't just Amy and me anymore.

"Do you worry about the baby?" I asked as offhandedly as I could manage.

"Sure. From the stress though as much as anything. The hours are going to be long, especially until we can get a full staff hired and trained. And we'll have to do a full publicity campaign. Also, we need to have some carpentry done in the house to get it ready. We need an internal wall and a door between a couple rooms. Do you think you and Steve could do that?"

She was already in, turned on, lit up with the thought of the job.

"You'll be in the spotlight. In the *Bonner County Daily Bee* probably, and later testifying in court against some of those guys," I said, thinking about how radically conservative and sometimes violent northern Idaho can be.

"Yeah. And we're going to do trainings with the sheriffs and city cops."

"You'll be known as the woman responsible for Sandpoint's women's shelter."

"There's an executive board, and my boss, the executive director," she said, but I caught a glimpse of her smiling in spite of herself. She's wanted to start such a place since those days when she first worked at the Harbor House, and at just twenty-seven years old, she was getting the chance. I wasn't about to stand in her way.

"I think Steve and I could come in and take a look, get a materials list together for the wall and door."

It was a perfect morning, bright as only winter can be, the sun shining off every snow-bent limb, off snowbanks as high as our truck, off snowpack on the road itself. As we drove across the long bridge over Lake Pend Oreille into Sandpoint, the water and mountains and sky flashed in our eyes and we had to squint to see. We sang along with Eric Clapton, his steel guitar through the truck's speakers as clear and bright as the day. This can be a brutal life we are bringing our baby into, and there is little we can do to offer protection. But, as Amy hit the high notes on "Layla," I knew that our baby would be born to a mother who doesn't cower before or ignore that brutality. Our baby's mother would be a fighter, a woman unafraid, who sings in the sun.

Chinook. In Idaho the word means a warm south wind. Lately, it is the dirtiest word I know.

The snow was up to forty-six inches of accumulation on open ground, two inches shy of four feet in nondrifted areas, the most beautiful snowpack you can imagine, fluffy and dry, perfect for our daily skis around the ranch, when the powder would part around our ankles like air then close over our tracks behind us.

Roofs around here had feet of snow on them. Even the ranch outbuilding roofs we'd shoveled a week before had accumulated another couple feet. The drifts around our cabin were up to the eves on either side so that the front door looked like the entrance to a snow cave.

Beautiful, but dangerous. Three days ago the wind turned. It came up from Mexico and California, picking up speed through the deserts of eastern Oregon and southern Idaho. The Chinook. The warm southerlies that hit here almost every winter. But this is no ordinary winter; this is a record year for snow. And, since the rains came with the wind, all that big, light snow has become a sponge, soaking up the weight of the rainwater and holding it in place.

Roofs have begun to collapse—the Sandpoint High School auditorium, a warehouse, barns, and houses. The National Guard has been called up from Boise and Lewiston to shovel roofs. My own knees are sore from days of shoveling. Everyone in these mountains is hellbent on the same goal, *shovel the roofs!*

Amy and I were feeling smug. I'd been shoveling away with others on shallow-pitched roofs until early into the morning and drinking beer or cocoa inside when we'd finished, relief spreading over the faces of the grateful occupants as they put drink after drink into my tired hand. But Amy and I built our roof steep and covered it with metal to shed the snow loads of just such a winter as this. Snow never accumulates more than a few harmless inches. We were prepared and safe in our home, thinking we'd get through it unscathed. Until I heard the sound of gurgling water.

It had started New Year's Eve, sometime between 12:15, when we went to bed, high on our kisses and resolutions, and 4:00 in the morning, when I got up to feed the woodstove. I heard the sound and shone the flashlight down a narrow gap between the floor and the wall where we plan to pour the footing for a rock wall behind the woodstove. The light sparkled back from the surface of the water just inches down. I didn't wake Amy to tell her, but I spent the rest of the night lying in bed, listening to the sound of water trickle into the shallow space beneath our floor joists, a creek running under our cabin. That, and the sound of more rain on the roof. More rain.

When I went down to check behind the woodstove at six, the water had risen another inch, about three inches from the surface of the floor. I went back to bed terrified, feeling like a failure and an idiot for building our floor so low, virtually at ground level. When we built we had no machinery to lift the logs, just an improvised, risky system of ramps and pulleys. Amy wanted to go higher with the log walls, but I gritted my teeth with every enormous log, some thirty feet long and twenty inches thick, that rolled up into place.

So we settled for a low cabin, low walls, low floor—snug. A snug cabin for our new family.

Now, if the water down there freezes, if this Chinook ends suddenly before the pool has somehow drained, the foundation could heave. The floor joists could crack and bow. The ground could chew up months of work in an afternoon.

By nine in the morning New Year's Day, it was forty-five degrees, but the rain had stopped. Amy slept in and I went out front and dug in the snow until I'd made a trench running down hill from the front wall. The trench quickly filled with fast-moving water, and the stream continued on downhill under the snowpack toward Westmond Creek.

Digging the trench was something to do, and it felt, momentarily, better than sitting around, thinking up a list of disasters that could ensue and waiting for our dream to crumble under our feet. Seeing the water rush away from the cabin was satisfying. I was sure the trench must be doing some good, preventing even more water from pooling up under us. But an hour later the water level down there hadn't fallen yet.

When Amy got up and I told her about the water, she rolled up our new living room rug to haul up to the loft in case the flood did run over the floor. We were expected down at my grandparents' for a New Year's Day meal and a toast to our baby-on-the-way and our new home, and we decided we might as well go. If the cabin was going to flood, it was going to flood and there was nothing more we could do. I prayed that it wouldn't, though, that our child would grow up to see this little house as we've seen it, solid and snug and dry, standing among the quaking aspen for the rest of her life.

Rain. More rain last night. Rain slowly melting the mountainous snowbanks, toppling the wave-tip curls of drifts, streaming off the roof. Rain running under our house.

The water level under the floor is up another inch or so. The trench I dug in the snow downhill from the front wall is still a quick little stream. Since the water level has risen so little, I can only conclude that water is flowing out as fast as it is flowing in under the cabin.

Steve is a part-time contractor who has built perhaps a dozen houses. He assures me that at the very worst the foundation will sag in the downhill corner where the water exits, a problem we could fix relatively easily this summer by jacking up the logs and shimming under them. He's assured me the cabin is *not* going to collapse in on itself or slide downhill as I've been imagining it might as I lie awake in bed.

47

Our home will come out of this okay. It must. I keep picturing the dust-dry earth under our floor this coming summer, the log walls and foundation solid and unmoved. Our baby is growing inside Amy, growing with the inevitability of the earth tilting our northern latitude back toward the sun. This cabin is my gift to people I have not yet met and, after them, to people I will never know. Besides a few bookshelves and decks, it is the only thing I have ever built with my own hands.

The rain falls. The snow melts. The stream under our floor gurgles on. Our baby grows. We wait.

I feel as though that rivulet of water is carving its way across the surface of my heart.

I have driven the five miles to the View Cafe to get off the ranch, away from the unseen current under our cabin and the nervous, unseen currents running through my family down at their houses. Everyone is moody there today, holed up against this slop. It's too wet to feed, so the cattle wander their tramped path scrounging for strands of yesterday's soggy hay. Today is a good day to be off the homeplace.

The View is the closest restaurant to the cabin, and they serve breakfast all day. It's a tiny, narrow place, with a worn wood floor, pine paneling, and rural scenes painted on old cross-cut saw blades hanging here and there. There are only a dozen tables. The woodstove I remember from my childhood has been replaced by baseboard heaters that are kept comfortably warm. You can sit in that warmth for hours and look out the window at Cocolalla Lake across Highway 95 and listen to the loggers and log truck drivers and ranchers talk over their steaming plates of steak and eggs.

Across the lake, pine and fir climb the backs of a couple low mountains. Since the Chinook, snow has fallen off the trees, and their clean, wet greens deepen to blue higher up and further away.

Beautiful as it is, though, this country is hard and that hardness shows on the faces of the people who live here. The head waitress at the View Cafe—I'll call her Kathy—has a small smile she'll flash only for a moment when you thank her as she delivers your plate. Her eyes are tired, deep in her face and dark. Six weeks ago, toward the end of our string of November blizzards, I heard that her husband shot himself and died in the little A-frame they lived in next door to the café. I'd seen him in here, but we'd never spoken. I wouldn't presume to guess why he did it.

What I do know is that Kathy was back waiting tables in a week. In a few more days her notice appeared in the *Bonner County Daily Bee*, thanking all her friends and coworkers and customers for their support during her time of loss.

I am generally frightened by grief, apt to keep my distance and turn my eyes from the ashen faces of the mourning. There is such unbridled power in their sorrow. For a while, they know something the rest of us don't, something I don't want to know. Still, I wish I had known Kathy well enough to say something kind and more relevant than "Everything was delicious."

The longer we are here, the more I am beginning to realize that to belong someplace you have to suffer some of its losses. You have to mourn a little with your neighbors. You have to invest yourself in an environment that, like any environment, is constantly threatened and eroding. There is no other way home.

In October one of our heifers gave birth to a late fall calf. The cabin was still not finished enough to keep out the weather, and Amy and I were still staying at my uncle Steve's big log house. Amy had left for work, Steve was out feeding, and I was

49

rebuilding the woodstove fire on a pile of the previous night's embers. It was cold, the first deep cold snap, well below freezing. The fire recovered and climbed into the kindling, and I was warming my hands as Steve burst through the door with a newborn calf in his arms and shouted, "Run a warm bath!"

We put the calf in the tub, and it lay there shivering, the water turning a reddish brown from the blood and manure in its coat. Its nose and ears felt like they'd been in a freezer, dead already.

"She must have been born in the snow sometime last night," Steve said, taking off his stained chore jacket. "I don't think she'll make it."

We soaked the calf about fifteen minutes, holding its underbit chin above water as it slipped in and out of consciousness. Then we toweled it off in front of the woodstove. "Do it like this," Steve said, rubbing the towel roughly over the calf's back, "get the circulation going. Don't be timid about it." He was acting automatically, and suddenly I saw in him the man who's been thirty years at raising cattle.

"Don't rub her head though," he corrected me as I worked my towel up the calf's neck. "Don't want to rub off the birth smell or the mama won't take her. In fact . . ." He picked up his chore coat, covered with birth mucus, and rubbed it on the calf's face.

The little calf began to pick up its head a bit in front of the fire, and I could feel the warm blood returning to its nose and the tips of its ears. Steve told me that calves need to start ingesting mother's milk within the first few hours of life to get the extra antibacterial ingredients that the mother cow produces initially. In the orange-tinted colostrum she gives the first few days and weeks is the extra boost that calves need, especially this calf, to ward off infections like pneumonia.

But ours was a first-time mama. She was clueless. When we

placed the calf on the snowy ground in the midst of all the ooze and blood of her birth, the heifer walked over to her baby, sniffed it a bit, then walked back over to her flake of hay.

The nurturing instinct can be unbelievable in some cows, which have been known to nurse lambs and colts. Our milk cow, Gramma Bossy, is like that. She's the mother or grandmother of most of our herd. She gives so much milk that last year she lost a teat to mastitis, a disease of overproduction. Despite painful injections of penicillin, which made her dance around in her stanchion, gangrene set in and a quarter of her bag fell off. According to Steve she nursed the entire time. The pain from her calf instinctively thrusting its snout up at her udder must have been excruciating, but her drive to motherhood was so strong that she stood there and took it and let down milk in her three remaining quarters.

When Gramma Bossy saw this new calf lying in the snow she came trotting over to it from fifty yards away. But something kicked in for the new mama heifer, who lowered her head at Bossy and backed her away from the calf.

The heifer's protectiveness was a good sign, a great sign. But that was it. When Gramma Bossy wandered away, the heifer went back to her hay. "She needs to nudge it, to get it standing up," Steve said, "or it's gonna die."

I walked over and picked a bunch of bloody mucus up off the snow and rubbed it on the calf's forehead and over the thick curly hair on its back. The heifer, "Shorthorn" as we call her based on her daddy bull's bloodlines, is a grazing cow. She's never been handled and spooks and trots off when anyone gets within about twenty feet of her. Which is exactly what she did when I approached her and her calf. But when I was done she trotted back and sniffed and even licked the calf a bit.

Steve hadn't said anything when I'd done it, just watched. I suppose he'd figured by that point I couldn't make things any worse than they were. If the mother kept neglecting the calf, we'd have to bottle-feed, and the calf's chances of survival would drop significantly. Now, seeing the mother take a new interest in the calf, he whispered to me, "Good job."

But the interest was brief. Soon Shorthorn was back at the hay, and the calf was beginning to shiver on the ground. I walked over to them again, and again the mother trotted off and eyed me warily from a short distance. This time I lifted the calf up onto its spindly legs. It fell forward onto its chin. The mother let out a low, grunting moo. I lifted the calf again, and this time it remained standing.

When I backed off the mother trotted over, and things really went well. Shorthorn put her nose up under the calf, sniffed the dangling umbilical cord, and even lifted her baby a little when it wobbled. The calf fell. The mother turned away again. "Damn it," Steve and I whispered simultaneously.

I crept back over and lifted the calf again, and again Shorthorn took a brief interest. We went through this four or five times, and each time the mama's interest held a bit longer. At last the calf took a few tentative steps toward the udder. "Go! Yes," we said under our breaths and clenched our fists. "Come on!"

The calf passed right under the cow and fell down on the other side. I was blind with frustration. I wanted to jump and kick the snow, screaming obscenities.

We decided to set up a watch. We carried the calf into a small, sheltered corral and lured Shorthorn in with a grain bucket, though she seemed anxious to be near her baby and took little coaxing. Here the calf would at least be sheltered from the wind, and the ground was dry and not covered with snow.

I brought out a chair, a wool blanket, a thermos of cocoa, and a newspaper and settled in to take the first shift. I looked the part of some die-hard sports fan, sitting in a lawn chair in the snow. Except that I was surrounded by a dozen indifferent cattle.

No progress for the first hour. I took Yukon for a walk in the woods and came back to relieve my cousin Jeremiah, whom my uncle had awakened to take the second shift. Jeremiah said things weren't good. He explained that the calf had been down the entire time and was shivering badly. He left me there in the chair and went inside to make coffee.

Again, my instinct or impatience or simple irresistible human urge to interfere with nature took hold, and I impulsively climbed over the log-pole fence and into the corral. Shorthorn gave a moo and scrambled over to the opposite corner.

This was before we learned Amy was pregnant, before I knew I was about to become responsible for my own baby. Since finding out I'm going to be a father, I've become less reckless. I don't drive the gravel county road home from Westmond Store fast anymore, with the headlights out and only the flashes of moonlight between trees to see by. I'm going to leave my coiled rock climbing rope hanging on its nail on the wall this summer. When I go up on the barn roof to shovel off the snow, I stay back from the edge now and toss my shovelfuls instead of walking up to the brink to push them over. Knowing I'm going to be a father, I certainly would not climb into a small pen with a relatively wild, easily spooked, new mother range cow and try what I tried.

I got down on all fours and wrapped my arm around the calf's neck, like you would do to a wrestling opponent. Tugging it beside me I crawled toward the mama. My chest tightened so I could barely breath, but I forced a whisper. "That's it, mama. Yes. We're gonna just come right over and get this baby nursing. Yesss. Yesss. That's a good mama. Good . . ."

The calf bawled suddenly and the mama scrambled to the corner of the pen, then, realizing she was trapped and hearing the calf's bawl and seeing my arm around its neck, turned toward me and lowered her head. Despite being named Shorthorn, she has no horns, so my attention was focused on those hoofs and the thought that she would stomp me into the manure and straw.

I stayed where I was, afraid to move if even to jump up and run. The calf squirmed under my arm. Shorthorn stood there eyeballing us with her big, rolling brown eye.

"Good mama," I finally forced out. "Good mama." I stayed there on all fours with the calf for many minutes. Finally, Shorthorn began to relax, turning her attention out toward the other cows over the fence. She paced along one side of the corral and back to her corner. She was eight feet away, her udder hanging in perfect position.

I crept forward slowly until I was right up next to her, an arm's length away. Her eye turned back at us, and she gave a long moo of complaint. But she didn't move, at least until I reached out my hand for her udder. She began backing out of the corner, and I grabbed for a teat.

The moment my hand made contact she froze.

"Good mama," I said, amazed as she just stood there allowing me to squeeze forth a stream of milk. I'd never even milked before and am sure I must have been doing it poorly, squeezing too hard or not enough, but there it was, milk. I crouched down, completely vulnerable now if she decided to kick a hind leg forward at me or stomp me with a front hoof. I got right under her and pulled in the calf.

It took some fumbling as the mama stepped forward then stepped back nervously, but I got the calf's mouth open with one hand as I held it around the neck with the same arm. With the other hand I pushed the teat in and squeezed.

Milk dribbled down the calf's chin. I had no idea what I was doing. For all I knew I was going to choke the calf, get milk into its weak lungs and make it sick, or I was going to kill it from exhaustion, or mess up its natural nursing instinct by forcing it. All these seemed likely, if I didn't get trampled first.

The calf squirmed and fought my forced nursing. The heifer danced around a little. When I figured I had a cup or so of milk in it, I let the calf go and crawled backward, crab style, to the other side of the pen.

I sat there, the butt of my quilted coveralls soaking up piss and manure and mud. The calf stumbled and sat down on the ground. Shorthorn, however, stood in place, seemingly ready to continue.

After a few minutes waiting for the calf to get back up, which it didn't, I crawled back over and placed my hand on the heifer's teat and milked her a bit, the steaming milk pooling on the sloppy ground as I stroked her side. Without breaking the rhythm, I reached over, picked up the calf, and put its mouth on the teat again. Again, most of the milk streamed down the calf's chin.

Suddenly, the calf closed its mouth around the teat and took a suck, then another. Along the inside of my elbow where I held the calf's neck, I could feel it swallow, and I heard the unmistakable sound of more sucking as it took more of the teat into its mouth. Its underbit lower lip gripped higher and it arched its neck to get up under the bag. I let go.

I sat in the opposite corner of the pen, watching them, my butt and knees wet with their stink, my hands sticky with the milk now passing between them. The calf's tail swished as calves' tails do when they nurse. I was watching the oldest story play itself out again for the trillionth time. I was dizzy and weeping.

I watched them in the corral, the calf nursing, Shorthorn

mama patiently standing there, letting her milk down, until the calf fell over. I stayed for maybe an hour, but its belly was apparently full and it never got back up on its own to nurse.

When I walked back in the house and told Steve what I'd done and everything that had happened between the cow and the calf and me, he was quiet a moment, then smiled a deeply satisfied smile and said, "That's nothing short of amazing."

For the next few days I went out every couple hours to start the calf nursing on Shorthorn. Both cow and calf grew calmer and more accepting of my presence. So I would keep smelling to the cow and calf of their own bodies, I let my overalls go unwashed, and the canvas was soon crusty and stiff. The calf looked stronger each time I went out, and each time it took less convincing to nurse.

On the fourth morning, I went out to perform my part and, turning the corner around the barn, glimpsed the calf nursing. It had started on its own! I crept back away before either calf or Shorthorn saw me and silently raised my arms in victory.

Steve said that was it. The calf, despite big odds against it, would survive. It would probably grow into a great milking cow, tame and gentle from having been handled so much. It would certainly have a deep trust of me and would recognize my voice and touch, Steve said with a grin. Steve wants to keep this way of life going, wants to keep the family in ranching. I suspect that for Steve, this victory was as much about me as it was about the calf.

The next night we watched the movie *Twister* on video. My cousin Heidi was home from college for the weekend. Her brother Jeremiah and sister Jennifer munched popcorn on the sofa beside her while Amy and Steve and my aunt Marguerite and I tipped back in recliners. All of us sat in the dark, surrounded by that seven-bedroom log house and the woods beyond, and watched tornados chew up Oklahoma. I imagined we looked like some contemporary version of that TV family the Waltons, who gathered around their living room to listen to the news of the war and comedy shows on their vacuum-tube radio, which would whistle and crackle over the broadcast voices.

Halfway through the movie, as a tornado ripped apart a drive-in screen, Steve pulled himself away long enough to check the animals. Though he didn't tell me until the next morning over breakfast, it was then that he discovered the calf, "Chancy" as we had that day decided to call her, lying stiff and cold on the ground in the pen, dead for no obvious reason.

I'm sentimental. I admit it. Sometimes the whole world seems to spill over with meaning and emotion and lessons. I had never before seen myself as particularly capable with small, weak, new life. Truth is, I've always been reluctant to hold babies, made nervous and awkward by their dependence and vulnerability. But I'd gotten involved with something small and, to a point, had been successful.

It wasn't long after the calf died that I found out we were going to have our own baby. I knew I was ready. But I knew also, the world does not care what I know. Or what I want.

The Second Trimester

Oh might I here
In solitude live savage, in some glade
Obscured, where highest woods impenetrable
To star or sunlight, spread their umbrage broad,
And brown as evening: cover me ye pines,
Ye cedars, with innumerable boughs
Hide me, where I may never see them more.

— Adam in John Milton's *Paradise Lost*

T wenty thousand years ago, during the Great Ice Age, a finger of the polar cap extended to point south through the Purcell Trench Valley in the middle of what is now northern Idaho. The north-south running glacier, the Purcell Ice Lobe, blocked the course of the east-west Clark Fork through the Cabinet Gorge, where the mountain walls rise straight skyward from both sides of the river.

With no way around the two-thousand-foot-high ice dam, the river backed up, filling the gorge and the Clark Fork Valley behind it all the way east to what is now Missoula, Montana, and creating a lake that held half the volume of water that currently fills Lake Michigan. The lake eventually rose higher than the ice and began overspilling and slowly eroding it. Then, all at once, the weakened dam collapsed and released a cataclysmic flood that roared over the Pend Oreille Basin and down over our small Westmond Creek Valley, covering the ridge on which our cabin now sits with hundreds of feet of water on its way down to the wide Rathdrum Prairie and through the Spokane Valley toward the Columbia, hellbent for the Pacific with a current ten times that of all the rivers of the world combined.

Now, as I hiked up to the cabin from Uncle Steve's, where Amy and I had retreated so she could get out for work in the morning, it felt like the great Spokane Flood had come again.

The ice of our own small ice age had given way and released its little torrents all around us. Our half-mile driveway had become impassible by truck. The sides of the narrow swath in the snow that had been plowed open so many times were above eye level in places. And the little canyon of a road was filled knee deep with rain and meltwater that stung cold as it drenched my jeans and seeped into my boots.

At the cabin the surface of the water down in the opening behind the stove shone in the flashlight beam. The flood was two inches below our floor. One inch higher than it had been when we left in the afternoon.

Outside, the stream out our front wall flowed down the trench I'd dug in the snow, relieving at least some of the pressure on our homemade, cinder-block foundation. The air had cooled a little. I clicked off the flashlight and the water gurgled in the dark. If the temperature dropped a little more the melting would slow, but if it got too cold that pool under the floor would freeze and expand.

Back at Steve's house, Amy and I sat up watching TV and reading by the bright lights, trying to enjoy the comforts of electricity. But our minds were on that stream running under our house, and television shows and microwave popcorn weren't much distraction.

Around nine, Steve left for the Westmond Store. Fifteen minutes later the phone rang. Westmond Creek—which runs under the county road right where it ends and our ranch road begins—was about to overrun the bridge. He said we'd better get our pickup out right away, that the creek was rising fast and the road would be impassible in a matter of hours, if not minutes.

Normally, being stranded on the ranch or even all the way up at the cabin is no problem. The county road has been snowed closed a half-dozen times this winter already, and we've welcomed the chance to hole up and write, ski, work on some of the interior carpentry, and wait for the plow (which has never been more than three days and is usually here in one).

But in the morning, Amy had to get down to Coeur d'Alene for her last day on the job at the psychiatric hospital. It was a Thursday night. If she missed Friday, she'd have to go down Monday to finish up and get her belongings, missing her first day at her new job at the Sandpoint women's shelter. I drove down the road and didn't park until I was a quarter-mile past the bridge and a good twenty feet of elevation above the creek.

In the morning, Amy and I walked down to the truck hand in hand. Though it had overrun the road by eight or ten inches, the creek flood was slow moving enough that we could walk across it like a couple school kids in galoshes, our pant legs rolled, dry shoes and socks in our backpacks. We drove the county road to where the creek crosses under it again. At this second bridge from the ranch, the water level hadn't risen above the four-foot culvert pipe, though it was within inches of doing so and was moving much faster.

I rolled down my window and we watched the creek flowing deep, wide, and angry through the meadow. Some of that water had run under our cabin and now was headed for Cocolalla Lake and Lake Pend Oreille and eventually, like the Spokane Flood twenty thousand years before, for the Pacific Ocean.

I hadn't been to the cabin yet to check the water level, but there was no reason to think the flood under our floor was any worse. It wasn't raining, so the only water flowing under the cabin would have been meltwater, and it got cold enough late in the night that there shouldn't have been too much of that. If the rain held, we'd be okay.

Still, sitting in the idling pickup above that culvert pipe, feeling the road tremble from the rush of Westmond Creek beneath us, I felt small and powerless. For the first time in a long time, I felt threatened by this world. It was easy to believe that we—me, Amy, our unborn baby, all of us—could be washed off its face as if in a deluge of trees and mud and chunks of ice and endless miles of water.

One month to the day after we learned we're going to be parents, I did something I'd been meaning to do most of my life but had never gotten around to. I went to a Quaker service. But "service" isn't exactly the right word; "meeting" is what it said on the sign on the community church across from the little Sandpoint Post Office. "Friends Meeting."

And the people inside did look friendly. They were dressed casually in wooly sweaters, blue jeans, and boots, and they glanced up and welcomed me with nods and smiles as I stepped through one of the well-worn wood double doors.

The meeting was like being alone in the wilderness. The hour felt like three blissful days. We sat in silence, our chairs in a circle at the front of the plain chapel, an hour of silence with a couple dozen strangers, quiet as a ring of unspeaking mountains around a hidden valley. It was like walking out into the alfalfa field behind our place. No voices pressed back on my mind, so my mind stopped pressing, my brain went slack, began to quiet itself in the midst of the enormous, answering silences around it.

If God was in that church, He was a little creek running down between mountains, a cold, bright creek speaking in tongues, or a wind. Not that *I* could hear anything. But I resolved to go again next week.

The Chinook was over. The temperature was back down in the twenties. The water beneath our floor had been falling an inch every two hours, and that morning I hadn't heard even a trickle flowing in under our back wall. North Idaho belonged to the province of winter again.

The cool-off was at the center of the conversation at the potluck after the Friends' meeting as we piled our paper plates high with cheeses and pineapple slices and pecan pie. (This was an important part of church I'd been denying myself— good eats.) Most of the Quakers live out in the mountains, on roads with names like Rapid Lightning Creek and Upper Pack River. Like me they were relieved that the temperatures had dropped and that the rain and melting had subsided. I suppose part of the reason I'd come to church was gratitude that our home hadn't washed away and that the creek running beneath it had dried up. We knew we'd face high waters again in the spring, but we'd been granted a reprieve, like the rest of the congregation. For now, all our bridges and foundations and steep, narrow roads would hold.

Unlike the grace of the mountains, our human states of grace are transient. Peace passes away or is crowded out by our busy voices. Even so, I want our baby to know a lasting peace.

I want to learn patience. Most every night I wake up and stumble outside to take a leak—one of the benefits of living without plumbing. It is always there, the silence in the smell of woodsmoke drifting down from our chimney. Silence all the way across the valley, and into the next valley and the next. The world listens for the creeks to ripple and the wind to pass through the trees.

We heard the baby's heart beat yesterday. Actually, it was more of a swishing sound, quick little swishes, the first of billions I suppose. In all likelihood, that heart, still smaller than my pencil eraser, will be beating long after my own heart has stopped and cooled to the temperature of earth.

I opened my eyes and handed the headphones back to Amy. She was lying on the examination table, the microphone against the clear jelly on her abdomen, her head turned toward me. Tears were welling up in her wide, green eyes.

"We won't be alone anymore," she said.

This was Amy's big, week-twelve appointment at the Sandpoint Women's Health Clinic. Before the exam we met Gena, who is to be our nurse-midwife, in her office. She is older than Dr. Bowden, whom we'd met at Amy's first appointment a month ago, but like Dr. Bowden, Gena was dressed in the comfortable, outdoorsy style of so many women in the West. In her denim dress, tiny turquoise bear earrings, sandals, and long graying hair, she looked the very image of motherhood.

As she and Amy talked, Gena leaned in and placed her hand over Amy's hand now and then and explained things like nutritional fiber and pelvis size and prenatal stress. These are strong, magical people, it occurred to me—Gena, who has witnessed and facilitated the births of hundreds of human beings, and my own wife, who was even now joining the ranks of motherhood.

Gena turned to me. "The more you can make healthy eating, exercise, and stress reduction a part of both your lives, the better your experience is going to be. Prenatal care is really a couple's issue. What questions do you have?"

"None yet," I said. "I just think it's amazing, though, that men have been outside this whole process for so long. What a shame."

Amy patted my knee. "He's very enthusiastic." She smiled at me, "That's good. It feels like we're in this together. That's very important to me."

"You bet it is," Gena said. "So, let's talk about the conception."

I sank into my chair and let my eyes wander up over the dozens of photos of babies above Gena's desk as the two of them talked about possible dates of our baby's conception and compared those dates with Amy's menstrual cycles. Though I was sure it happened on a certain warm, early October evening up in a place called Carlson's Field, not far from the cabin, as the moon rose over Butler Mountain, I wasn't about to join the conversation.

But I wasn't leaving either. Embarrassed or not, I wasn't going to be anywhere but with my wife, who was nodding and laughing with this sage of a woman. And when they stepped into the exam room, I had a pretty good idea I'd be mortified half the time, but I was going to hear every word that was said.

With what I thought might be the slightest furrow of concern across her brow, Gena told us that Amy's lower uterus was bigger than she'd expected for a pregnancy only twelve weeks along. Perhaps it was simply that Amy was small, she explained, and the baby was growing big. "Like its father," Gena said and winked at me. Or maybe, despite all their frank talk about our love life, Amy was further along than we'd calculated. Or, she told us with a grin as she washed her hands in the steel sink, it could be twins in there. *Twins.*

If there were other possibilities, Gena didn't mention them, and any expression of worry I might have seen on her face had gone as quickly as it had come.

Next, Gena took out two pairs of headphones and put one on. She squirted clear jelly from a plastic bottle onto Amy's belly, rubbed the microphone around there listening for the heartbeat, and explained that we may or may not hear it today, and that one often can't hear a second heartbeat even if there are twins.

We breathed tiny, silent breaths. We wanted to hear a heartbeat, a sign that our baby was doing okay. Gena stopped the microphone in one spot, smiled, and said, "There it is."

While Gena kept on one pair of headphones, Amy and I traded the other pair back and forth. We must have looked like giddy adolescents hearing the long-awaited album by their all-time favorite band, or people living at some distant outpost listening to the news from home. Anxious for her second turn, Amy watched my face for reactions.

The only sound I've heard that reminds me of that tiny swishing heart, picked up and amplified through the electronic microphone, is the sound of pulsars, the most distant bodies humanity knows of in the universe, heard by a field of giant radio telescopes in the Arizona desert. Both sounds have traveled unimaginable distances to reach us, both are as old as time, the echoes of the beginning of creation.

After hearing our baby's heartbeat, we left the clinic high, and we were high all afternoon, smiling at each other and holding hands, having heard a magnificent secret together.

But by night the words of the woman in the clinic's billing department—words like "payment plan" and "installment" and "services performed"—began to reverberate in our skulls, the obscene noise of the world crowding out the music of that heart.

We lay in bed awake, running the numbers, which has practically become a habit.

"Compared to most people around here, we're rich," I said. Amy did have to swallow a 20 percent pay cut to take her new job as the director of the shelter. And this pregnancy certainly falls under that perverse, insurance-company-bet-hedging category of "previously existing condition." But truth be told, between a grant I received to write and Amy's salary, we are loaded by native north Idahoans' standards.

"Thirty-four thousand combined. Twice the starting pay

for a teacher in this county," I added, as if just saying the figure out loud made it enough.

"And still, somehow we're in trouble," Amy answered.
"We'll have to slow our spending on the cabin to only a couple hundred a month if we're going to be able to cover the payments the clinic wants and stay up on the credit cards."

"We needed those credit cards to get this place as far along
as we could this fall. To beat the snow."

"Yeah. And we still don't have windows in or running water
or kitchen cabinets or anything to cover the insulation in our
ceiling."

"I know."

The baby is due in six months, maybe sooner, Gena had
said.

Amy and I always try to reach some resolution to our trou-
bles and kiss good-night before we close our eyes and drift off,
even if the resolution is temporary and the kiss just a peck. But
it was well after midnight, and we had only silence left for each
other. We weren't even angry, just emotionally spent, sunk
down in the wake behind our earlier crest of elation.

As we lay there with our heads on separate pillows, I was
beginning to realize why most people only daydream of cutting loose to move up to the mountains or back to the old family farm and build a simple cabin. Perhaps for the first time in
my life, I understood how easy it must be, how almost inevitable, to sink into a life of well-paying if unrewarding work
broken up by a week or two in some lakefront cottage or time-
share condo six hours of freeway from home.

I could feel money, like sand around my ankles, pulling at
me to stop, to give up, to stand still.

Progress on the cabin, the first progress in a couple weeks. The triangle-shaped, front-gable windows we'd ordered (and paid for) weeks ago finally arrived, and Steve and I installed them, standing precariously on ladders, holding each big, heavy window in place while fumbling to hammer in the flanges around the frames before the whole window could fall back on us.

Progress on the cabin is good for my heart, but it's essential for Amy's. All the other windows may still be covered with tightly tacked plastic on the outside and blankets hung by finish nails on the inside, and we may not know how we're going to get the money to do anything about that, but this morning Amy woke up in the loft and looked across the vaulted ceiling above our little living room and out those two, big glass triangles. For the first time, instead of fogged-up, sagging plastic, she saw the valley falling away from us then rising again into Butler Mountain.

A fresh snow dusted the trees.

From this day on we will wake to the weather, to that mountain through those big, twin glass triangles.

I rolled out of bed early, stoked the stove, and stepped in my bathrobe and mukluks into a clear, cold dawn. Halfway down the snow-packed path to the outhouse I saw fresh, unmistakable elk tracks. This one had been a single animal, bigger than the elk whose tracks I'd seen before. This was a bull. He'd been twenty feet from us as we slept. With no electric lights bleeding into the dark, no drone of television, no chatter from a clothes dryer exhaust, our dark, quiet cabin must have seemed no particular threat.

When I went back inside, Amy was up in her bathrobe and sitting on the little footstool in front of the woodstove. I told her about the tracks, and she bundled up in her coat and boots, grabbed her camera, and followed me out. She crouched down right next to one of the prints, pointed her lens at it, cabin in the background, took a picture, and said, "Proof it was that close to us."

Then she looked up and for a moment seemed to be studying the forest where the tracks led. Was a part of her thinking of following them? It wouldn't have surprised me. She's becoming a woods woman since we've been in Idaho.

Or, more accurately, even more of a woods woman. After all, it was Amy who gave me skis for my nineteenth birthday and taught me to use them. And before that, in high school, it was her family canoe—an old Grumman aluminum they'd had since she was in kindergarten—that we used to take up the Dead River north of Marquette. We'd stop on our way to the put-in beach and buy a small boxed pizza and a two liter of Coke at Luigi Brothers' Take Out then eat the pizza cold an hour later, sitting under the pines on some little island in the river and passing the bottle of Coke as a heron slowly high-stepped through the grass on the bank or a swimming cormorant slipped beneath the surface and reappeared somewhere else, swallowing his meal.

It was Amy who taught me the names of those birds. She'd been born in Marquette, the daughter of an outdoorsman father with no sons, and though they lived in town, she went out with him hunting or fishing or getting up firewood or just scouting every chance she got. "Lady bird beetle," she'd correct me when I'd say "lady bug." When I'd use the word "pigeon" she'd say "rock dove." Though she'd never killed anything and never wanted to, she'd fired a rifle many times. I never had and still haven't.

But it wasn't a hunter's steely squint Amy had on her face as she looked into the timber where the elk tracks led. It was a

71

slight smile of admiration, the face of a woman who wants to see and name and know everything she can about the world around her.

In our bathrobes, winter coats, and mukluks though, neither of us was exactly dressed for tracking. And maybe there were a few things to learn about the world *inside* the cabin, I thought, as I looked from that lovely face down to the skin of Amy's shin and knee where one of her legs showed between the wooly cuff of her boot and the flannel hem of her robe.

I crouched beside her and put my arm around her shoulder.

"Wanna go in?" I asked, slipping my hand up along her neck and giving a little tug at her earlobe—our signal since those early days.

"Sure."

Amy and I came to Idaho in part because we wanted ownership, and now that we're here I've found myself questioning just what ownership means. I chose this spot for my home when I was twelve years old while out walking with my grandfather. When I told him it looked like a good sight for a house, he carved my name and the date into a quaking aspen that still stands, now right next to the cabin, and still bares the grown-in but readable scars: *Jon's sight. June 29, 1979.*

The closest neighbor was Slim Carlson, whose dairy farm shared a property line with our land. Like the rest of the neighboring places, his house was far off, but the closest part of his property to the cabin sight was his forty-acre hayfield just up the ridge.

Slim bought his entire place in 1937 for three hundred dollars he had saved cowboying as a ranch hand in the Dakotas after immigrating from Sweden. He built all the log buildings, including the small barn on the hayfield near us, by hand. He cleared the hayfield from a small meadow, every year or two cutting a few feet back from the thick wall of white pine, Doug fir, and larch that ringed the pasture, and he used a horse team to get out the logs and pull a stoneboat, a flat sled for clearing rocks. There are three stacks of field rocks out there at this very moment, each stack as big as a house.

Carlson's Field is an amazing place, the highest point on this side of Westmond Valley. June mornings when I was a kid and would return here for the start of my summer visit, I'd pour cold milk on my breakfast cereal from the big, wide-mouth jars Slim sold it in. When I was done eating, I would hike up to the field through the waist-deep hay. The mountains would rise up from the woods below me until I topped the hill. At the very crest of the field, mountains would rise all the way around me, so close I would spread out my arms and imagine I brushed my fingertips along the peaks and ran my palms along the soft ridges.

When Carlson died and the field came up for sale a few years ago, Amy and I were poor students, living in Kalamazoo, in southern Michigan, scrounging in the car for laundromat quarters, bumming beer money from friends whose student loan checks had come in early, and before we or any of the rest of my family could come up with the cash, the field sold.

I was devastated. Worst of all, it sold to Billy Strand, a man who had for several years been known locally for buying up land on the cheap, logging what valuable timber there was on it (which Carlson's field had—a beautiful ring of timber around the clearing), and subdividing it down into ten-acre parcels that sold for three or four times per acre more than the original price.

And sure enough, as soon as he'd bought it, Billy had the thick, dark woods that Slim had left around the field thinned out, cashing in on tens of thousands of dollars of prime, century-old and older timber.

Thankfully though, he still hasn't listed lots for sale up there. Not yet.

I admit I am guilty of terrible greed when it comes to land. Our ranch already has a beautiful alfalfa field, right behind our cabin. And my uncle now owns another eighty amazing acres of pasture a few miles from here, and we graze cattle in the summer on his mother-in-law's ranch just down the road. For an unemployed writer, I am absurdly blessed with land to ski and ride horseback over and hike and just sit on.

But I covet that field. I want to own it so my child can wander up there as I have, and so that child's children can, and their children. I want them all to know that place where the world spreads out below and rises again, the horizon soaring with the Monarch and Selkirk and Cabinet Mountains around them, their fingertips tingling to reach across and touch.

Any yet, sometimes when I'm up there alone, my heart pounding from the climb, my nostrils and lungs full of the same sweet air Slim breathed for most of his life, when that magic is working, I know that this place is forever, that in one form or another, it will outlast me and outlast Billy, as it outlasted Slim. I know this place will outlast my carved name on that aspen beside the cabin. And I know that the ownership I want for Amy and me and our baby has little to do with whose name is on what deed or even what tree and has everything to do with love.

Uncle Steve saw the elk. The other day he banged on the cabin door and burst in wide-eyed to tell me. "I saw 'em, Jon. I saw 'em."

I knew what he meant instantly. My uncle is forty-seven, but in his expression I glimpsed what he must have looked like as a boy, eyes still wide with his vision of wild creatures.

"They're probably still up there," he continued, at last catching his breath. "Two cows and a bull. Back in the timber at the edge of Carlson's Field. They didn't seem the least bit spooked."

I didn't bother to change out of my blue jeans and cotton denim shirt, or even find a hat. I threw on my skis and set out for those upper pastures.

When I topped the ridge the mountains soared around me, as they always do up there, but the elk were gone. I skied over to the tree line, and sure enough, there were deep hoof prints everywhere. The tracks wandered around the trees, through a couple bedded-down spots in the snow, and off down the hill into the deep woods.

Patience and passivity have never been strong points with me. Persistence and willfulness, sure. You want something forced—a stuck vehicle, an environmental cause, a deep-rooted stump—I'm your man. But I can't stand to sit and wait, helpless to do anything but hope. I'd like to learn a little repose, to learn staying power and quietude from these mountains. I want to be ready when my baby is born to shed a layer of will and move into the next part of my life, fatherhood, clean and smooth.

The nineteenth-century philosopher William James spent years studying religious experience, interviewing self-proclaimed mystics and prophets, reading biblical, poetic, and philosophical accounts of grace and transcendence. One of the traits he found such experiences have in common is passivity. Buddhist or Hindu, Christian or Atheist, when the spirit of creation takes you, it *takes* you. You can make yourself ready for grace. You can fast or smoke peyote or read the Bible or walk into a field of broken corn stalks in autumn, but grace will come only when it will. Grace cannot be earned or attained. This is what the Quakers know and why I am attracted to them. No one speaks until the Spirit moves, and until It does, they wait. The only way is to be still and open.

As I stood there, though, staring at those elk tracks, my will took over. *Forget William James,* I thought, *I'm seein' me some elk.*

I tracked them for hours, skiing through thick brush, my glasses fogged and my ears numbing. I got reckless, skiing down steep, dense woods, whipping by three-foot-thick trees miles from home. I'm not an especially coordinated back-country skier. I can't carve wide, graceful telemark turns or flip my weight from ski to ski to slow my descent, and the elk tracks went down impossible grades. For a while I was reduced to walking downhill sideways on my skis, painfully slow progress as the elk got further and further ahead.

My skis were loud on the crust of the snow. I was frustrated to be making such noise, *crunch-swish, crunch-swish, crunch-swish*, every time I moved. But I would have gotten no place in snow that deep on foot. I made a mental note to track animals on snowshoes from now on.

I followed the elk tracks all the way down one thickly timbered ridge then through curves and circles until they doubled back . . . and crossed my own ski tracks that I'd laid not ten minutes before!

They'd been that close, keeping tabs on my progress and merely avoiding me, in no rush to escape. They knew I was no real threat, but they weren't going to be seen. They'd yield nothing to persistence.

The tracks crossed my own twice more as I struggled back up hill, falling in the snow several times and huffing from exhaustion, making no attempt at stealth anymore. When I finally returned to Carlson's Field it was snowing hard. The wet flakes slanted with the wind, down across the field, and collected on my glasses and sweaty hair. I stood for a few minutes and looked back into the timber, the green so dark behind the snow it seemed black.

I still have plenty of city in me. I want my experience, and I'm willing to work for it, to go get my heart's desire. There is joy in cities, but it is most often deliberate, premeditated joy— you choose your off-ramp; you stand in line for your takeout Thai food.

The mountains aren't like that. The mountains give their gifts like grace. The mountains are bigger than us. They will not be had.

I gave up tracking and just stood in the falling snow. Nothing I could do. Nothing to do. Nothing. I pointed my skis down the long, sloping, open field, hollered like an idiot, "Hey elk! Hey!" knowing they could hear me, and let go to the effortless speed of downhill.

Dishes. Amy and I pour water from five-gallon storage jugs into pots and kettles we warm on the woodstove. When a steady plume of steam rises we pour the water into washtubs in the sink, one to wash, one to rinse, and put more water on the stove. When the wash water gets cruddy with bits of food and the rinse water gets foamy with suds, we pour them down the drain to buckets under the sink, buckets that, when we are done, I will carry off into the woods and dump. We start over with fresh hot water from the stove and repeat the process, three or four times if we've let a couple meals' worth of plates and pots and silverware stack up. It takes us maybe twice as long as it did in that life before the cabin, and we pass the time talking.

It was dark outside and the dishes were from a rare, late-evening dinner of linguini with red clam sauce when Amy led us into the subject of where and how to have this baby. In the soft light from kerosene lanterns, I washed and rinsed as she dried and stacked. She was explaining to me that she wanted to rethink our decision to go back to Marquette a couple weeks before the delivery.

"Really? I thought you'd want to be surrounded by your own family. Plus, my parents are there," I said.

"It would be familiar and we'd have good support. I'd love to have my mom there," she said. She held a bowl in her hand and stared into it for a moment, as if she could see her mother inside. "But I'm also thinking about how much time we'll have there once the baby is born. If we go back a couple weeks before my due date, we'll have less time to be there after, with the baby, which is what I want most."

Amy has three months of maternity leave and could, theoretically, work right up until the baby is due.

"But are you going to want to go in every day to work nine months pregnant?"

"Sure. That's not even a consideration for me. I'd much rather be occupied than just wait around, even in Marquette. I'm just going to want every possible day with the baby after the delivery. I don't want to waste a day of my leave."

Three months of freedom to give herself over completely to her child, to walk the floor with that child, to lie in bed and watch that child sleep, to hold that child and dance in the sun. I can see why she wanted to save up every minute of it.

But I had gotten used to the idea of us bringing this baby into the world in that tiny city where I knew that somehow it could hear and feel the waves of Lake Superior a few blocks away, and taste in its first breaths the air that even in July blows down from the Arctic over that cold, fresh water. Amy was right, though. If she's going to go back to work full-time—and it looks like she'll have to, at least for a while—then she should save all of her precious leave time for mothering.

"We'll have to tell our folks," I said, dipping a plate in the rinse water, the ceramic warm in my hand. It was one of the plates we'd gotten as part of our wedding set of dishes, a plate with bright colors—orange, green, blue, and yellow in concentric circles, a few chips knocked off around the edge.

"I know," Amy said, taking the plate, toweling it off, and stacking it, still warm, with the others down in our single cupboard under the counter. "But they'll be glad for all the extra time with their grandchild."

"So we'd leave a couple weeks after the birth?"

"Once the baby is ready to make the trip."

"You really want to have this baby in Idaho?"

"I'd love to deliver in Marquette, but doing it here will be good, too. It'll make the whole process more ours, just the two of us."

"I'm surprised."

"The baby'll have an Idaho birth certificate," Amy said.

"I'm glad you feel that rooted here."

"I do. Also," she sat her dish towel down on the counter while I scrubbed a pot, "I've been thinking I really want to deliver here. At home."

"In the cabin?"

"Yes. I think so."

She'd mentioned the idea before, had even had information sent to us by area midwives, but she hadn't brought it up since we'd decided to go to Marquette for the delivery.

"We're a long ways out, at least a half an hour from the hospital," I said. "I don't know if they could even get a two-wheel-drive ambulance up here. Plus, the road's so narrow."

"It'll be summer. The lumber truck got up here fine in the summer. That was a two-wheel drive."

She'd thought this through.

"What about electricity?"

"What about it?"

"I don't know. And a telephone. Shouldn't we at least have a phone?"

"We can get a cell phone," she said. "I just want to feel like I'm in control. I don't want some doctor swooping in at the last minute to run everything right at the finish line. Doctors are more apt to do episiotomies."

I'd known that. She'd read to me from one of her pregnancy books weeks ago that, statistically, physicians more often do that procedure, which involves cutting the opening of the birth canal to enlarge it and move things along.

"I want the birth to be on my terms. In my own space."

"What about Dr. Bowden's practice? They have great midwives who are nurses too, like Gena."

"And everyone there seems kind and patient," she agreed.

"Right, not people who'd push you around."

"But when you deliver you don't get a say in who attends. You get whoever's on call, no matter who you prefer. And they say you have to deliver in the hospital. I asked."

Amy's courage stunned me. My wife—who I sometimes worry I've lead into a harsher life in these mountains than she'd envisioned—wanted to have our child in this small, remote, unfinished cabin.

I'm selfish. I want to keep her with me, don't want to risk any harm coming to her no matter how small that risk, and no matter if I have to chuck my self-reliant ideals. I can't imagine, looking back on it, how she could have let me go out the door back in those early days of our relationship when I used to climb mountains and cliffs. But then, she's never needed control over anything more than herself, never imagined, as I have, that she could force her will on the world.

I told her that my job was support staff and that the decision had to be hers ultimately.

"You're my partner though," she said and wrapped her arms around me from behind, me with my hands up to the wrists in dishwater. "I'll be okay. We'll do it here, together. And we will have a midwife. They have done this before."

"A baby, born here, in this cabin. Can we at least get a midwife with an RN? Maybe one from Coeur d'Alene or Spokane would be willing to make the drive if no one in Bonner County has one."

"Sure. I really will be fine, you know."

"So you're the rugged one after all, the self-reliant mountain woman. And your man's the wimpy city boy."

"Hardly," she said with a squeeze.

My grandfather has a saying. I don't know the story behind it, but he says it whenever he wants to tell you that only you can decide how you want to conduct your life. "It's your hay, Ed," he says and chuckles, looking right into your eyes.

Amy'll have the baby in the cabin if that's what she wants, and I'll do everything I possibly can to help. Even get out of the way.

We took down the remaining plastic and blankets and put in all the rest of the windows. More debt. But last night, as Amy drifted to sleep, I stood in the living room surrounded by the light of a full moon on snow and pine, moonlight lighting the sky above the dark crest of the mountain, moonlight pouring in and filling the cabin, exactly as I had known it would since I can remember dreaming.

Driving the county road just past the old Hollingsworth farm (which has traded hands four or five times since Hollingsworth died), I passed two semi trucks with low-boy trailers parked alongside the road while a bulldozer and a backhoe plowed up the snow and dirt in the woods. They were carving a new driveway back into the cedars and tamaracks that grow thick and dark along the road through there. Another driveway.

Summers, when I was twelve and thirteen, I'd drive our forty-year-old tractor through those woods, pulling a flatbed stacked high and wide with bales of alfalfa hay from Hollingsworth's fields.

This is still the wide-open Idaho mountains. We still can't see a single light from our hilltop cabin at night. Elk wander by right out our front door. Compared to the vast majority of American people, we live on a rugged, mythic landscape. But change has happened faster around here—more houses have gone up, more roads have been built, and more trees have been cut—in the last twenty years than in the half-century before.

In the black and white pictures from his youth, my father stands with his three younger brothers and my grandfather in front of a flatbed Ford truck loaded down with a day's work worth of eight-foot stud logs, all cut with crosscut saws. The boys mug for the camera—sleeves rolled up, felt hats pulled low, double-bit axes on their shoulders. The youngest, my uncle Richard, is seven or eight. He holds a ceramic gallon jug to his lips as if it were full of moonshine. My grandfather stands, arms folded, above and behind them. They are all living in a land vastly bigger than themselves, a land seemingly impervious to the changing power of human activity.

I was born some ten years later, that winter when the closest phone was at Art Evans's place, a mile away, and Art took the call and hiked from his farm through the December wind to the bottom of the field beneath my grandparents' house and hollered again and again, "It's a boy! It's a boy! You have a grandson!" over the half-buried fences and snowdrifts until my grandparents came out to the porch and waved to him and called back, "Yeah! It's a boy!"

These are among my myths, the history I inherited and imagined in the upstairs, low-ceiling bedroom of that farmhouse as I watched the moonrise over a valley filled with ghosts.

Now, as the bulldozers cut the latest new driveway and the well-drilling truck rolls in, I worry that those ghosts will not stay, that they'll be driven over the mountain and will not whisper their wild love in the ear of the next Johnson. And I wonder how many more pieces of this place will fall away before my child sees it.

Standing at the pay phone at the Westmond Store, I made my weekly call to my folks in Michigan, and Dad told me some news. "Some real bad news with Mac," he said and paused, giving me time to get ready.

Mac is a long story for me, a novel even. He's a psychologist my dad's age, and we've been counselor and client, fellow writers, even rivals for the affections of the same waitress once when Amy and I were broken up briefly in college, and for many years now he and I have been close friends. I braced myself to hear what had happened to him.

My dad told me that Mac's sixteen-year-old son, Shaun, and three of his high school buddies had been killed on the highway just outside Marquette. It was in the late morning, before a weekend basketball tournament. They were rounding the rock-cut along Lake Superior, heading east out of Marquette to get one of the boy's birth certificates that he'd forgotten at home and had to have to play in the tournament.

The boys found themselves on ice—a frozen breath of Lake Superior spray that frequently makes that spot a hazard. Those of us who have driven the road for years know the ice is often there. We ease off the gas and slow way down in winter when the mist-tossing waves are up. We are vigilant, on guard for that floating, slow motion feeling when the steering wheel seems to disconnect from the tires and the brakes become useless. We drive cautious and slow. If you've driven northern roads for a few years, you develop a sixth sense about ice, you know when it's beneath you. You slow way down, then test the brakes and sure enough, the tires don't grab.

But those boys were new to the road, laughing maybe and zipping past a slower moving car when the road let go of their tiny Geo and sent them sliding across three lanes and head-long into the path of a town-bound semi.

I imagined Shaun waking up early, leaving that big old house of Mac's in sweats, the cold washing over him when he opened the door, basketball tucked under his arm.

Mac drives an antique BMW motorcycle and writes fiction. His stories are filled with a counselor's insight and kindness, but the empathy in them is balanced by a kind of midlife-male sexiness, an urgency and speed, his prose opening up and racing away from you full-throttle and loud as that old BMW.

When I'm back in Marquette I run into him often while walking the Lake Superior beach two blocks from his house. He always looks boyish and satisfied, strong but contained with the lake breeze on his face, a little like Alan Alda I've often thought. Now, nothing the world can ever do will make things right for him again.

The morning after the phone call it was another perfect day in the mountains. I opened the cabin door and walked out onto the hard crust on the surface of the snow. There was no depth to the sky, just blue light above the highest golden green tips of the trees. No hint of wind.

I'm going to be a father myself. The odds are with me that

fatherhood won't come to inconsolable, unimaginable suffering. Odds are that being a father will forever be like walking on the thick crust on top of four feet of snow in the cold, February sunlight. Until that phone call, I hadn't even imagined it could be otherwise.

In addition to feeling deeply mystified and sad for Mac, I am a touch afraid. My love is branching further into the world than it ever has, further into time, beyond my own life.

Amy is a hardy soul, tough even. As a kid she wanted to play hockey and is still resentful of the rules that prevented girls from playing in leagues from pee wee to high school. She's slept on the ground beside me countless nights and carried a seventy-pound pack for days. So when she said her knees and hips were aching only a few hundred yards into a hike, I was surprised.

"We'll go back," I said, trying to hide my disappointment. We'd driven the rutted road that winds up the Pack River Valley into the Selkirk Mountains north of Sandpoint, all the way to the end of the plow route, where we'd parked and set off down a snowmobile trail on foot. "We at least got a look at it up here."

"I'm sorry."

"No, no," I said. "What I mostly wanted was just to be up here. There's nothing much different ten miles in, I don't suppose."

It wasn't completely true. In fact, I'd had the faint hope that we'd catch a glimpse of one of the last thirty woodland caribou in the contiguous United States. The small herd frequents the upper reaches of the Pack River Valley.

We stopped to turn around and Amy said, "Listen." Through

the quiet where our boots crunching on snow had been, we could hear spring in the rush of the river to get more snow down out of these mountains. Spring was eating away at the snow and breaking ice loose from the riverbank, swirling it downstream.

When we'd walked a ways back, Amy said, "You really wanted to get up there, didn't you?"

"I did. But this is good."

"It's not much of an adventure."

"Maybe I'm ready to rethink my definition of adventure," I said. I'd driven a heap Oldsmobile from Chicago to Central America, where I'd sat alone on a beach at the edge of a jungle and cut breadfruit into bite sizes with a machete. But somehow this short, slow walk beside my pregnant wife was better.

Amy squeezed my hand and stopped. For a moment I thought she was in trouble, that she was going to tell me she'd felt something new and dangerous in her abdomen. But instead she pointed through the cedar boughs at the river and said, "Look." A small bird, a type I'd never seen before, blue-gray and plump, was standing on a sheet of ice on the river. It plunged in, head first like a penguin. We could see it underwater, darting along the gravel riverbed for a long time, until it finally popped back out and onto the ice.

Neither of us had even heard of such a bird.

"Maybe it's hunting some sort of water bug, something that hatches really early," Amy speculated. "Or maybe a tiny fish."

"We wouldn't have seen this if we hadn't turned around," I said.

Amy was quiet a moment, then said, "You're going to make a good dad."

We stood silently watching the bird dive and swim and surface only to shake its feathers and dive again, until the cold

crept through our boots and we walked the last few steps to
the truck.

I don't want to write this section. I want to keep on writing
about settling into these mountains, about nesting in our new
cabin, Amy and me holding hands, giddy with this pregnancy. I don't want to admit that fear has crept into this story that
seemed so blessed.

The day after we took our short stroll in the Pack River Valley, we woke in the cold and sunshine that filled the cabin and
walked suspended along the crust of the surface of the snow
over parts of the ranch Amy'd never been before, along the
east fence line—where the elk tracks showed us that the herd
had stayed on our side, as if knowing they were welcome—and
over onto the area we call the Back Slope, a dense woods where
dark cedar and white pine have been left unlogged for most of
a century to grow thick, tall, and straight.

I want to keep writing about days like that, and about how,
when we got back to the cabin, we stole up into the loft and
made love, then snoozed away the afternoon, wrapped in each
other's arms. But we've learned that those days of unbridled
optimism and unworried joy are over.

The ultrasound was going well. The young, friendly technician dimmed the lights and the machine lit up like an air-
craft instrument panel at night. Right away she saw one baby
(no twins, a pang of disappointment). As she moved the ultrasound around on Amy's abdomen, the screen showed us a
head, an arm, even kidneys.

Amy and I held hands as the technician pointed out,
through the abstract gray haze, a tiny foot, less than an inch
long. All the while the technician commented how things
looked very good, the baby healthy and complete. I was having

a difficult time making anything of the images on the screen, could hardly discern the baby from the fuzz around it. It was like being told by someone there is a giraffe visible in the shape of a cloud and not being able to see it.

Suddenly, the baby moved, and I saw it all—the tiny hands on either side of the head, the curled legs. I pointed to the screen. "Is that an ear?"

"Sure is," the technician answered and smiled, pushing a button to record the picture for us.

She kept sliding the ultrasound sensor over the clear jelly on Amy's lower belly. Then she stopped.

She held the sensor still and pushed buttons that amplified the view of that spot. "Your cervix is a little open on the inside," she said and pointed to a dark sliver in the center of what should have been a solid white cone.

My heart began to creep up in my chest as the technician began to work intently, pushing buttons on the machine, rotating the probe, looking for a better angle.

"And this baby's a little low. Nothing to freak out about," she began, "but I want to have the radiologist take a look."

Within two hours we were sitting in the obstetrician's office exam room. Dr. Bowden sat on the little sink counter in her skirt and tennis shoes and looked back and forth at Amy and me. She'd just finished giving Amy a pelvic exam.

"Well, I'm worried," she said and sighed.

We nodded and listened and asked questions as Dr. Bowden explained how Amy was carrying this baby low, and that Amy's lower uterus was stretching, threatening to pull open her cervix. Dr. Bowden talked about premature babies and trying to first get past the twenty-fifth week—the low end of viability when the baby would need weeks or months of intensive care—then past the thirtieth week, then the thirty-fifth and into the safe zone. Amy was seventeen weeks along.

"What are the odds this baby won't make it at all?" I asked, wanting the whole picture, wanting to know exactly what we're up against.

"Twenty, maybe thirty percent," she said.

Twenty or thirty percent. Between one in five and one in three. I lay in bed that night, trying to get a handle on those numbers, but they kept taking shape, turning to giant block letters in wild colors—purples and oranges, children's colors—and sprouting wings and flying away from me.

Dr. Bowden said Amy had to be on bed rest. The idea was to take the pressure off her uterus, to try to get the baby to take up residence higher. The distended cervix wouldn't get better, she told us, but it could hold together fine as the baby grows and moves (hopefully) higher up. Amy'd been having pains low in her abdomen all along, and now she was to keep a journal of them in an effort to find a pattern. The hope was that the pains were the *result* of these problems, not contractions that could be *causing* the problems.

Bed rest.

As the director of Sandpoint's domestic violence shelter, which was still in the hectic start-up phase, Amy said she'd come to think of her work as essential. Dr. Bowden said for the time being Amy could go in a little bit, as long as she worked reclining. No sitting up or walking around. Back at Steve's house Amy called her work and explained all the changes she'd need to make in her routine.

Amy's staff is made up of wonderful, kind, generous women. They work for a few bucks an hour to ensure that other women and children have a safe place to go when the world comes crashing down on their heads. So I wasn't surprised when Amy's secretary called back later and said the staff had all talked and decided to volunteer additional, unpaid hours to give Amy time off. Still, over my mumbled protest, she went in the next morning with her sway-back deck chair to put in a couple hours.

Because we have no phone up at the cabin, and because it is so isolated by our barely passable road, we decided to move back down to Steve's house. My uncle and aunt's generosity was superhuman during the whole time we were settling in here and building the cabin, and I will always be grateful to them for that and for encouraging us to move back in with them after Dr. Bowden prescribed bed rest. But the thought of staying with them again also made me feel trapped, afraid we'd become fixtures in their place with no couch of our own to curl up on together, no quiet time in our own space, no snoozes in front of our own fire.

I went back up to the cabin in the dark to get our pillows, some books and clothes, and Yukon. It was starting to get cold. The fire had gone out hours before.

I sat on the loft steps and listened to the propane lantern hiss. Everything—our unmade bed on the loft floor, the box of cedar kindling I'd recently split, the bowls we'd left on the kitchen table after breakfast—all of it seemed to be waiting for us to come home, filled with optimism and plans, as we'd done so many nights before.

Yukon came halfway up the steps and stood there, his tail swishing slowly from side to side. I scratched behind his ears. He'd been alone since morning.

Amy goes back to Dr. Bowden's office for another exam in a week. If, at that time, the decreased activity level seems to be helping, Amy will be able to do a bit more—though the hikes and skis and long afternoons of lovemaking are clearly over for the duration of this pregnancy. I'll ask if we can move back up to the cabin, provided we get a cellular phone and Amy is not there alone without me and the pickup. But if her cervix isn't holding on its own, if the baby hasn't moved into higher territory, we could be looking at complete, strict bed rest. No work. No cabin. Maybe even hospitalization.

We are under siege. We're all but certain that Amy's new insurance will consider the pregnancy previously existing, and now our medical bills will probably double, *if* the baby makes it to full term and needs no special care. I've decided to give up my full-time writing schedule and look for paying work.

I catch my mind constructing scenarios alternate to the one we're in. If we'd stayed in Kalamazoo, Amy fully insured, our folks a mere eight-hour drive away in Marquette . . . If I'd taken a teaching job at some university where Amy could recline comfortably in our college-town apartment and I could slip home between classes to fix her lunch . . . We are paying big dues to live here, and they're about to get bigger. More and more I can see why so many people our age only dream of abandoning the security of cities and budding careers to move far out into wild country.

At the bottom of all this, when I whittle my worry down to its core, is my love for our baby—the little creature we've been calling Bean after the size it was when we first learned Amy was pregnant. Of course, our baby isn't even a baby yet, but a fetus. No memories yet, no experience—just warm darkness. And pure potential. Potential that has transformed our lives, opened us to parenthood.

When we call her, my own mom describes my dad standing at the kitchen window watching children sled down the hill at the school across the street. Up until her activity was limited, Amy would stop off on her way home from work and buy one-piece outfits, fleece and cotton, with prints of polar bears and ABCs. I feel this enormous, new capacity for tenderness. Often Amy pats her abdomen and her mouth lifts into a smile on one side when she says, "Bean's getting hungry," or "I talked to Bean today."

The very possibility of loss seems like an obscenity now.

Two days after the bad news, Dr. Bowden's office called with some potentially good news. Amy's culture for the streptococcus bacteria came back positive. An expanding lower uterus and separating cervix are symptoms of this particular bacteria. Apparently, after a cervix has started to separate, it won't normally go back to its former shape for the remainder of a pregnancy, even if the trouble was originally a reaction to the bacteria that's been treated. But, if the distention was solely the result of the bug, the distention shouldn't get any worse once the bug's gone. And, the implication for future pregnancies would be better.

Amy started a course of antibiotics, and she did well staying off her feet, lying in a recliner watching movies at Steve's house, using her sway-back deck chair at work. When I went to pick her up from the shelter, she was always reclining in her office, talking on the phone or holding papers above her head to read.

We didn't want to pin too much on the prospect that treating the bacteria would make everything fine, but we hoped. Still, I avoided looking at babies, heading for the dairy section of the supermarket when a mother pushed a cart with a baby carrier in it into the bakery. And there was a vaguely sad tone in Amy's voice and my voice when we made reference to the Bean's appetite or when we talked about our trip to Marquette to show off the newborn Bean in August.

We were ready to take any good omen, scientific or otherwise.

Then this morning, crossing the bridge into town, I saw another bald eagle in the same old, bare cottonwood where I'd seen one many weeks before. A friend of mine, who is a traditional Ojibwa Indian in Michigan, says there is no better sign than a returning eagle.

Amy and I were alone in my uncle Steve's house when she hollered my name from the bathroom. I ran and opened the door, and she was just stepping out of the shower. She was leaning with her hand on the wall.

"I'm dizzy. I'm so hot," she said as if talking to herself, water dripping from her onto the floor. She spun around and vomited into the toilet.

We agreed later that she must have stayed in the shower too long. Just normal pregnancy queasiness, we told ourselves.

As the days go by I've been watching over Amy, running down to Westmond Store for videos and 7 UP, cooking meals, bringing her blankets and pillows. And she's been patient, reclining in her big chair in that big log house of my uncle's. But we're starting to feel a little haggard and helpless, worn down like drifts of snow melting under the February drizzle that's moved over the mountains. All we do is wait, wait for the next doctor's appointment, for disaster or for the baby to get big enough to survive, whichever comes first.

"It's so unfair," she said, crying. She was sitting in the chair again, in her bathrobe, a towel around her hair. Her eyes were tearing up. "I rub my belly constantly. Every day I tell Bean it's too soon—you need to stay in longer. And now I won't get a home birth in the cabin. Now we'll have to be in the hospital, all sterile, and strangers will take care of me and the baby. God, I feel gypped."

All I could do was say, "Me too," and climb into that recliner with her and stroke her belly.

"So many women get to have a healthy pregnancy," she said. "They get to choose a home birth or the hospital. I feel like I must have done something for this to be happening to me. To us."

"You know that's not true."

"We've got to get some control back over our lives," she said. "We've got to get back into our own space."

"I'll try to find a used recliner to buy and get us a cellular phone so we can move back up to the cabin," I told her.

"Do you think we should?"

"I don't know," I said. "But either way it feels good just to think about it."

The baby was eighteen weeks along. Twenty-two to go to a full-term delivery. Eight or nine weeks until the third trimester and the point at which it could stand any chance at surviving on its own.

Milestones. We wait for milestones to pass.

But through the TV and long phone calls and magazine pages flipping by, it has become apparent that we shouldn't abandon our lives to waiting. Amy's determined to keep going in to work, even if it's only for a couple hours of paperwork a week and even if she has to lie on a couch or recline in her chair the entire time. At least she can still be in the world that much.

Though I'm tempted to go in with her and hang around the shelter, tinkering with a few carpentry projects so I can be there when she needs the radio station changed or a file from the file cabinet or a soda pop, she's discouraged me from doing so.

"Bowden said if I start to lose the baby there's nothing we could do about it. And I won't get up," she promised. "I'll have other staff there. You should work on the cabin. Keep focused on the big picture."

When Amy senses danger her tendency is to face it, to fight it out in the open. I freeze, try to blend into my surroundings and go unnoticed.

94

She was right. Whether we return to the cabin soon or wait, I need to get back to projects I've let go—caulking around the window frames, installing a propane cookstove, starting the cedar finish work so we can stop looking at so much exposed insulation. Optimism, I've come to believe, is just a word for all kinds of building. And what we want out of our lives here hasn't changed. We still want to bring this baby home to our own snug, little place. We still want to wake up early in the morning in the loft as the sun comes over the mountain and crosses the quilt and our baby's back, which rises and falls with the deep, even breaths of sleep.

We moved from my uncle Steve's house back up to the cabin today as the sun melted more snow. The road up was a mess of slush and ice, water and mud . . . too much mud for the end of February. I don't know how long the road will remain passable, but we made it today, the truck sidewinding and bouncing, tossing mud onto the hood and windshield. By the time we pulled up to the cabin the pickup looked like it'd been on safari.

We sat there for a moment. The cabin looked low and safe under aspen and fir trees, sun filtering down onto the green metal roof. The cabin is a constant. It has become a feature of this landscape. I wished I could be as sure of our fit in these woods.

Early this morning Amy had her appointment and Dr. Bowden gave us the go-ahead for this move. She said Amy's cervix hasn't gotten any more stretched open and the baby is higher up in the uterus. She wants Amy to keep work down to two or three days a week, lying down the whole time, but it's okay to keep going and okay for us to return to the cabin.

If things go wrong, if Amy starts to prematurely deliver this baby, Dr. Bowden said the extra few minutes it would take to get to the hospital wouldn't make any difference.

It was good to be back in the cabin, at first. I brought in the recliner Amy's been using, a loan from Uncle Steve, and positioned it in front of the woodstove where she could warm her feet in front of our morning fires. She got in and leaned back. I shone a flashlight down the gap behind the stove and saw the shimmer of water. But it was only an inch or so deep, nothing serious. We made our own trouble soon enough, though.

"Good news at the doctor's this morning," I said. But I could hear the doubt and fatigue in my voice.

"My cervix isn't any better."

"But the baby's higher up. And we get to be back up here, and you can keep going to the shelter." I climbed the stairs into the loft to unpack our clothes and make the bed as we talked, Amy downstairs, me upstairs.

"If I have to cut back any more though, the board of directors might not want to keep me."

"So let's just assume the worst?"

"I'm not assuming the worst. Why do you have to do that, jump all over me when I am just trying to be realistic?"

"Realistic didn't get us this far. I'm not jumping all over you. But what good does being down on our situation do?"

"We don't have any kind of plan. There's still all this exposed insulation. I don't want that stuff drifting down into the baby's lungs."

I looked up at the ceiling. The brown paper insulation backing sagged like flesh between the ribs of roof rafters from just above me in the loft to out over the vaulted ceiling above Amy in the living room. The words "Western Fiberglass" repeated themselves over and over in blue ink.

"Everything depends on my job," she continued, "which

is on very shaky ground. And how am I going to eventually stay home with this baby if we are totally dependent on my income?"

"Hell, I don't know. You want to just give up because we don't have the next two or three years figured out?"

"Don't shout at me!"

"I'm not shouting!" But I knew I was. From just feet above her I was hollering down. I didn't want to think about what would happen to us if Amy lost her job, of the bills that would mount and the grinding halt that would come to the cabin's construction. And I had nothing to say about after the baby was born, no clue how I'd ever make enough money for Amy to stay home.

Since getting the shelter job, she's said that she's willing to keep working for another year, though recently she's sounded less and less enthusiastic about the prospect of leaving our baby every morning. And I imagine she'll be all the more reluctant once the baby actually comes.

Lately, for the first time in two and a half years of marriage, I have no idea what to do next. I've gone to the Sandpoint unemployment office and applied for the few summer Forest Service and state park jobs posted there. But of course there wasn't anything stable or well paying. Work isn't hard to come by in northern Idaho—chaining up truck tires, bucking hay, fixing fence, cutting wood until your back aches so bad you can barely stand, shoveling snow from around vehicles and off roofs. Work is everywhere. Work that *pays*, however, is rare.

Even if Amy does hold onto the shelter job, my writing grant runs out in April, just when our medical bills will begin mounting. Between our student loans, impending medical bills, and the credit cards we racked up building the cabin, we need one good, full-time income. Despite the simple, electricity-less, rent-free life we plan to lead in the cabin, we would have a rough go of it living off anything I could make at unskilled labor around here.

"What do you want me to do?" I said as I struggled to slip an oversized pillow into one of our small pillowcases. My yelling had given way to that mock-resigned, whatever-the-hell-you-want-you'll-get tone that I end up hearing echo in my head and hating myself for minutes later. "Do you want to just leave here? Me to take some stupid janitor job in some city?"

"You know that's not what I'm saying. You know I'm not saying that. Just forget about it."

"Yeah. Great. I'll just forget about it!" I hollered and flung the pillow down on the bed.

I could feel layers of myself melt away. Generosity. The core of love must be generosity. My prayer is for selflessness. Not the mere back-rub, meal-fixing, bring-you-flowers-and-a-throw-blanket selflessness. That's easy. That's consideration, and (despite lapses, like this argument) consideration is second nature for me. I pray for the get-up-before-dawn, fix-my-lunch-and-leave-for-a-job-I-don't-care-about variety of selflessness.

Or, perhaps more accurately, the selflessness that would allow me to leave Idaho if that's what my new family needs.

I recently learned of a job teaching creative writing at a university in Oregon. When I told Amy last week, she asked me to go out and dig our old, dog-eared road atlas from behind the pickup seat. I brought it in and we turned to Oregon. La Grande, where the job is, looked like a good place—dry cattle country, so I've heard, sandwiched between two mountainous wilderness areas.

I imagined myself teaching college in Oregon, Amy meeting me at my office between classes for a walk with the baby, a little house somewhere at the foot of the mountains a half-hour from campus.

I will apply. I'm ashamed that I'm not keeping us afloat. And I want to work, to teach.

Still, mornings when I wake and step out into the cold air to feed the cattle or chop wood, I'm dumbfounded, *every* time, that I'm finally living here after a lifetime of longing. I want it all, want Amy to be able to stay home, want to live in our cabin with our baby, spending my days like precious currency on my love of words. Standing there in the loft, pillowcase in my hand, I was afraid of all I wanted, afraid of the hunger I have for this ranch, these mountains, afraid of the way I ache to stay.

We fell silent for a couple hours. As Amy napped I went outside and shook dust and sand from the area rugs and split and stacked a fresh box load of cedar kindling. The late sunlight slanted through the valley like a last-minute blessing. From somewhere through the woods behind me sunset burned against Butler Mountain, turning the green mountainside copper and giving detail to every tree on the still snow-covered ridge line against a bank of gray, towering clouds rolling beyond. It occurred to me that sometimes the lessons here are just that clear. And sometimes they are not.

We ended okay. We always do. When the cabin was again homey and neat and I was cooled down and Amy was awake from her nap, she said she wants very much to stay here. "I always have," she said to me as I pulled up the footstool and sat down beside her. "I just worry. I love my job and I love it here."

"Yeah well, I love you, Boss."

"I love you, too."

"I'm going to find a way to bring in some money before my grant runs out," I said, thinking how soon that would be. April. "I don't want you to worry if you have to quit. Or if you want to."

"I know," she said and held her palm to my cheek. "We can't forget we're in this together."

I put my hand on hers. "We're a team."

"All three of us," she said and led my hand down to her belly. "Do you suppose Bean heard any of that?"

"I hope not."

"We'll have to get better about our tones with each other," I said. "She'll learn how to handle anger from us."

"She's counting on us for a lot," Amy said.

"Joel's Fine Mexican Food," it says on the side of an aluminum panel van parked every day at the same corner in Sandpoint. I've become a regular.

"Señor," Joel smiled as I ducked under the awning and out of the wet flakes of falling snow. "What's happening with you today? You want the bean burrito for your wife? It's good for pregnant women."

I ate my burrito in the pickup and took Amy's to her at the shelter. She unwrapped the foil, releasing that heavenly smell, and looked up from the beach chair she parks herself on in her office and said, "The baby's been yanking on the cord for me to send down some chow."

"That's my baby," I answered.

Amy smiled. "Today, I'm really happy. Today, I want to keep doing this job and living in Idaho."

I bent down and kissed her and said, "We'll make it. Burrito comin' down, Baby."

I got the truck stuck where our road crosses the wettest part of the alfalfa field. A fresh layer of snow hid all the mud and hid my previous tire tracks, which would have shown me the driest way across.

Amy waited in the truck and for an hour I dug around the wheels. Then I pushed and swore, and finally, pounding on the hood with my fists, I gave up. She would have to walk down to my uncle's house, a terrible violation of her bed-rest orders.

I've started to ask myself if what we're doing is a bit foolhardy. To be honest, I'm becoming convinced it is. As I stood in shin-deep, cold mud, knowing every minute Amy had spent sitting in the truck increased the risk to our baby, and knowing how bad it was for her to have to walk down, I could feel defeat.

So, Amy and I will be house guests again, this time until the snow has melted off the hill road. Since we won't be driving up it and churning up mud, the road might be usable in a month or so if we get warm weather. Meanwhile, we'll be back in our room at Uncle Steve's ranch house, like a couple of flunky postadolescents who can't seem to get moved out on their own.

The following night, after Amy went to bed, I repeated my hike up to the cabin to get our clothes and pillows and toiletries. The fire had gone out and the cold had moved in again.

I snapped on the lantern and a low light sparked and brightened to the constant hiss of propane. Once more, nothing in the cabin hinted that the occupants wouldn't be home for the evening any time now. A bouquet of daffodils in full bloom on the windowsill, yesterday's cereal bowls on the kitchen table, our boots and sneakers lined up neatly beside the woodstove, all of it seemed to expect our return. Only the cold gave away that the place had been abandoned. Again.

I sat down in Amy's recliner. I was exhausted, caked to the knees of my jeans in mud from our ruined road.

I don't know how to write what has happened to us, so I will start with the weather. It began snowing hard late last night, wet snow that melted to slush as soon as it hit the pavement. By morning it had turned to rain. What saves any of us from grief that caves into our open hearts like silt? Not weather. And not the pewter, bare cottonwood tree beside the river out the hospital window. Not the crow that has been shuttling around in that cottonwood's tangle of high branches that bob under his weight when he lands and caws into the cold, damp sky. He has been cawing all morning.

What will probably happen in the next few days is this: Amy's bag of waters will burst and she will go into labor. Labor will be short, an hour or two, because the baby's only nine or so inches long. When the baby is born, it will almost certainly be alive, and it will survive some amount of time from a few minutes to several hours. At twenty or so weeks, its eyelids will not yet be able to open, but it (he? she?) will be able to hear and feel and touch. The baby will be capable of experiencing comfort and discomfort. Though it will feel pain as its unformed lungs gasp and struggle futilely to work, we will hold it and stroke it and speak to it until it dies in our arms.

I wrote that paragraph, maybe the most difficult one I've ever written, sitting in a vinyl recliner as Amy napped in the hospital bed beside me. How we got here is a story that starts yesterday afternoon in the dimly lit ultrasound room with the concerned tones of the technician and the big "U" shape on the screen where a thick mass of cervix should be.

Even I knew how wrong it looked, the dark womb fluids sagging and bulging there like an aneurism below the baby. The baby was so much higher in the uterus than in the last ultrasound, exactly where it should be, and head up now, not down as it had been. But the cervix . . . The technician roamed over Amy's swollen belly with the scope, and parts of the baby passed before the hazy gray monitor. The technician didn't know what tone of voice to use as she ran through her usual script of "there's a foot," "that's the baby's nose," and "this baby's really squirming around for us today." She managed a kind of mock enthusiasm, but her speech was too hushed, the silences between her observations too heavy. I held Amy's hand and we watched the screen without speaking.

The technician sent us to Dr. Bowden's office. Dr. Bowden consulted with the ultrasound radiologist who had reviewed the videotape of the test, and fifteen minutes later we were in a room in the Obstetrics Unit in the Bonner County Hospital.

At first the talk was of Amy staying on hospital bed rest for the duration of the pregnancy, four months if she made it to full term (a possibility we were realizing was becoming increasingly remote). Then, when Bowden came over to the hospital and examined Amy, bad turned to worse as we learned that Amy was now dilated between one and two centimeters. A contraction monitor was hooked up to Amy's belly and, yes, she was having contractions she hadn't felt.

Dr. Bowden sat on Amy's bed. She had changed into a light jacket and hiking boots since we'd seen her in her office. She's not much older than us, and she's already spent years practicing obstetrics in northern Pakistan, Mozambique, and inner-city Brooklyn. I knew she'd seen great suffering and loss, seen the looks on dozens if not hundreds of parents' faces like the looks that must have been on ours—looks of bewilderment and fading hope.

She spoke softly. She wasn't optimistic. She'd called the big perinatal clinic down at the hospital in Spokane. She'd spoken with her partner, Dr. Honsinger. Everyone agreed, things didn't look good for this baby. She'd give Amy medication in hopes of stopping the contractions, but the dilation was a big problem, exposing the womb and baby to the risk of infection even if the bag of waters didn't break, which it most likely would.

If the bag doesn't break, if the contractions stop for three or four days, if Amy doesn't dilate any more, and if infection doesn't set in, Bowden might be able to tilt Amy upside down so the bag slides back out of the cervix, pinch the floppy cervix together and put a stitch or two in to hold it closed. A desperate measure in which, of the host of things that could go wrong, the suture needle could bust the bag and initiate the delivery anyway.

Even if the delivery can somehow be delayed for five or six weeks, at twenty-five or twenty-six weeks' gestation the baby will have shaky odds of surviving and perhaps need months of neonatal intensive care.

Had we known Amy's cervix was so weak, Bowden could have put the stitch in early on, before trouble even started. But there is virtually no way to know in advance how a cervix will behave when first subjected to the pressure of a pregnancy. Now, with Amy already dilated, the procedure not only is likely to trigger delivery but may well result in a tear that could leave Amy infertile.

At midnight I stepped out to the parking lot to take Yukon for a walk. He'd ridden in with us in the morning, which—as I opened the truck door and pulled his collar on over his thick, sleep-disheveled fur—seemed like a week ago. For him too I supposed.

I walked him under the amber parking lot lights, his paws and my sneakers making perfectly defined tracks in the wet snow. Up on the second floor, Amy's light was the only one still on. I could see the ceiling tiles and curtain tracks, but I couldn't see anything else. If this had been another kind of night I would have thrown a snowball at that window, and we would have waved at each other, and Yukon would have perked up his ears as I said, "Who is it, Yuke? Who's that up there in the window?"

Before I left to walk Yukon, Amy was given a shot of a contraction-inhibiting drug. Bowden reassured Amy that it was a safe drug to use during pregnancy, but when we were alone in the room together Amy turned her head on the pillow, looked at me, and said, "I hope the drugs don't hurt Bean."

I crawled into that narrow hospital bed and wrapped her in my arms and wept at her goodness. I wept that she should suffer like this.

Last night I slept off and on in the recliner beside her bed. A baby was born a couple doors down, sometime after midnight. I could hear its mother groan.

Later, Amy woke me to help her use the bedpan. As she drifted back toward sleep she opened her eyes, gave a weak smile, and said, "The baby kicked."

All through the second day we watched paper scrolling out of the monitor, an inch or so a minute, a line indicating contractions in long peaks and valleys like a slow-motion seismograph. For a couple hours after each time Amy received the Procardia, her anti-contraction medication, the line flattened out a bit. But before long, and long before they should have, the peaks and valleys returned.

We'd been in the hospital close to thirty hours, but the contractions weren't going away. In order to perform what Dr. Bowden said was now the "far-fetched" procedure of stitching closed Amy's cervix, the contractions would have to calm right down with the drugs. Otherwise, the risk of the cervix tearing under the stress would be too great.

Dr. Bowden came in again late the second evening and examined Amy and again found her two centimeters dilated. The baby was still up high, good news. But that was to be the extent of the good news. The continuing contractions were the real bad news.

After Dr. Bowden told us this, Amy opened the door for a turn in the discussion. "What are we trying for?" she asked.

Before Dr. Bowden could answer, I asked, "What if Amy didn't dilate any more for the next few days? What will we have gained?"

Dr. Bowden spoke with a sad resignation in her voice, resignation and a hint of what seemed relief that Amy and I were ready for what was coming. "I admit I'm an indecisive person," she began. "I don't want to see you guys suffer for days and days as we keep this baby inside with Procardia only to lose it. Yesterday, I wanted to see what would happen. Today, I think we'd just be delaying what's inevitable."

Then, after a long pause, she added, "Trying to keep this baby inside is asking for trouble."

We'd lost. We could fight on, but the outcome wouldn't change.

No more drugs. No more monitor. No more bedpan. We'd let this come. And, we told Dr. Bowden, if it hadn't happened by tomorrow, we wanted her to give Amy a drug to help end it.

In a half-hour or so, Dr. Bowden was going to come in. It was noon, a little over twelve hours since we'd last spoken with her. Amy had not burst her waters yet, and so the plan was to induce labor to head off dangers of infection and end the torture. She'd be pregnant for another couple hours. Our baby would be dead by the end of the day.

Some white and black birds were floating on the wide, slow river out our window. Occasionally, they slipped below the surface and reappeared at another spot.

The crow in the cottonwoods that had haunted us the previous two days was gone. The wind was swaying those empty trees. Sun slid through the cloudy sky every so often.

We decided to donate any tissues that could be used, but we wondered what to do with our baby's body afterward. And would we name her? Should we simply call her Bean as we have all along? We wept and clung to each other.

Dr. Bowden arrived at 12:00 just as she'd said she would. She examined Amy and said that she was further dilated, to about four centimeters, and the baby'd moved down low. Delivery was eminent now. The drugs to induce that Amy was going to receive wouldn't be a direct cause of the delivery, but simply a facilitator to hurry it along. Somehow the difference, technical though it was, mattered to us.

Dr. Bowden also told us our desire to donate our baby's tissues was a tremendously generous and beautiful gesture, but that, by law, it couldn't be done.

When we were alone again, Amy and I talked about what to do with the baby's body. Amy said she wants to cremate it, take the ashes to Marquette and spread them into the cold water of Lake Superior from the cliffs where we were married.

"Yes," I said. "I think that's what we should do."

Soon Meg, the head nurse, came in and hugged us and told us she could start the i.v. at any time.

"A couple minutes," Amy asked.

"Of course," Meg said and left us.

I laid my head on Amy's belly and said good-bye.

Meg knocked softly on the door and stepped in.

"Ready?"

Amy nodded.

Meg hooked up the i.v. and turned the switch. We didn't cry or wail. I could hear the Burlington Northern rumbling by on the tracks across the river. The clouds had broken up and it was sunny outside.

Twenty minutes later, Amy felt contractions for the first time. They moved across her back and belly, like menstrual cramps, she said.

It was still sunny and windy out.

We'd been chatting quietly with Meg about her years in a cabin in the mountains east of town, holding our own emotionally. We were ready to have done with this agony.

We'd try to pick a name before the baby came.

When Meg left, Amy called her mother in Michigan.

I walked down to a freshly cleaned birthing room a couple doors down. A baby had been born in there the night before.

Out at the nurse's station two nervous, awkward teenage kids showed off their newborn to the nurses, who made adoring faces and spoke softly into the bundle of blankets.

Through the window of the empty room, I could see across the river and Lake Pend Oreille to the high snows on the Cabinet Mountains. The rich, thick clouds that had hung over us all morning were over the peaks, heading east into Montana. Along the opposite shore of the river, a young boy, ten or twelve years old, in a blue stocking cap and coat, walked along the frozen silt bank. I watched him walking, watching the river. A half-dozen ducks lifted off the water between us and turned together like conscious arrows toward the darker blue, choppy waters of the lake.

The next few hours we did better. We were relieved that the end had begun.

Dr. Bowden came in after visiting a delivering mom down the hall, gave Amy a quick check-over, told us the labor was progressing, then plopped down in one of the chairs beside the bed. We asked her how she was holding up.

"Me? I'm fine. It's you guys I'm concerned about."

"Yeah," Amy said. "But still, you look beat."

"Okay, I confess. Long day."

We asked her about herself and she sat back, deep in the chair, and exhaled. Grief-filled though our room was, Dr. Bowden seemed at ease with us.

She told us stories of her years in northern Pakistan and Mozambique. She said she'd come to Idaho and accepted her job in the practice because of a stray dog that the senior doctor had taken home and for which he was trying to find a new owner. When Bowden was in town interviewing, she'd met the dog and that was it. "I told him I'd take the job if I could have the dog."

Amy and I welcomed the distraction. Bowden's company reminded us that our own lives were, until recently, also adventure-filled and wonderful.

She talked about her new marriage, how it was an adjustment after so many years alone.

"I've always been fiercely independent," she said. "When I was a kid I was a tomboy, and I've never found someone I wanted to commit to. At thirty-nine, I figured I never would."

In her wire-rim glasses, short-cropped hair, green surgical scrubs, and hiking boots, she looked the very picture of independence. Since June she's been married to a widower, the Lutheran minister in Sandpoint, who has three teenage boys.

We talked about marriage and love. Every few minutes Amy rubbed her abdomen and lower back and said she felt a contraction. Bowden asked her to rank its intensity on a scale from one to ten. They were holding around three or four. When each one passed we kept talking.

Amy confided that I sometimes crowd her. "That's been one of the hardest parts of marriage for me," she said.

Bowden nodded and smiled at me. "I can see it," she said. "And it's the same for me. I'm a doctor for cryin' out loud! And Steve drives me to work, which is fine. But then he gets out and hands me my stupid briefcase. I told him it makes me feel like I'm in kindergarten." Amy and I chuckled knowingly. Though we haven't even been married three years, we felt like a couple of old hands.

"But we're good together," Bowden said as much to herself as to us. "He's this conservative, traditionally religious preacher, and I'm more of an Earth Mother–worshiping liberal, and we respect each other deeply."

She was quiet a moment, then said, "The biggest difference in my life is the male perspective. In my practice, it's all these women, all female energy. Like the shelter I suppose," she said to Amy. "But at home, it's my husband, these teenage boys, and their teenage buddies."

Amy told Bowden about the Johnson family ranch and all my father's brothers who grew up there and still visit often. "Masculine power permeates that place," she said.

Earlier that evening Bowden had left the hospital for an hour to watch the oldest of her new sons fight in a boxing match over at the high school. More guy stuff.

"He's a writer for the paper, not a tough guy at all, but intelligent and witty," she shook her head and laughed. "He does these things so he can write articles about them."

"How'd he do?" I asked with a grimace, feeling a bit of kinship with the young would-be pugilist writer.

"He's going to have a bruise across both eyes and the bridge of his nose for a week," she sighed. "But I think it was more traumatic for me than him."

Here we were in this dimly lit room in the middle of the night. Our baby was soon to be born dead, and this woman, our doctor, when she could no longer do anything medically, was helping to soothe our wrecked spirits with her presence.

And Bowden did another thing that helped Amy and me cope. We told her how guilty we felt for allowing ourselves to get stuck on the cabin road, and for the subsequent long walk Amy had to take to get out of the woods. Amy especially wondered aloud if she hadn't actually caused this. Bowden told us that, given how weak we now know it to be, in all likelihood Amy's cervix would never have held this baby to viability. She said it's natural to want to feel somehow responsible, that something could have been done differently and we are not powerless in the face of catastrophe.

"I feel guilty myself," she said quietly. She paused a moment before going on, then said, "I've been thinking how maybe I should have put you in the hospital sooner, kept constant watch over you. I'm such a positive person, maybe I wasn't cautious enough. What I'm saying is, it's natural to want to have an explanation. If I did something wrong, I'm not so fucking powerless." She sighed a long, empty sigh.

I realized immediately how vulnerable such an admission makes her. If only for a moment, Bowden placed our need for solace and reassurance above the safety of her own career. Amy and I will still feel guilty, I'm sure, probably for the rest of our lives, but as a result of Bowden's willingness to admit she's human and trust us with her self-doubts, we'll have the comfort of knowing we aren't alone, that our guilt is natural and not a sure sign that we have wronged our child beyond forgiveness.

How do I tell what I have seen? At 2:55 a.m., Friday, March 8, Hannah Marjorie Howko-Johnson was born.

She was born dead, a deep rose color, with bruises on her back and chest. She hung limp like Michelangelo's Pieta, the veins in her foot like veins in perfect marble.

We held her to our chests. She was long and slender, with thin toes and feet, and none of the baby fat of a full-term baby. Her eyes were still closed, and her face held the expression of a sleep deeper than I can imagine.

I performed a brief baptism, dripping water from a syringe on the baby's forehead. "I baptize you in the name of the Father, the Son, and the Holy Spirit, Hannah Marjorie Howko-Johnson."

Yesterday, when they learned that our baby would be born soon and very tiny, the nurses here had the hospital laundry alter a little receiving cape to fit her. They also gave us a fleece blanket with a teddy bear print. I am so grateful we will have these things to take home and keep.

We wrapped the cape around our baby and the nurse took her away for a birth photo and measurements. Dr. Bowden hugged us good-night, told us what a beautiful little girl our daughter was, and left.

The nurse returned in a few minutes with the baby and left the three of us alone. Amy held Hannah in her blanket, folding down the corner to kiss her good-bye.

Where was she? Where was my Hannah? It was so sunny. Someday, she would have wanted to play outside. Where was Hannah?

I didn't want to leave the hospital. It was as if our daughter were somewhere just a couple blocks away and if I watched for her out that second-story window long enough, I might see her pass between the trees. In these scenarios she was about five years old.

I knew that, after being with Amy through the delivery, my mind, the mind of a new father, naturally, *biologically* yearned to take care of my child. I knew that Hannah was gone, and any thought otherwise was not rational or grounded in truth.

I also knew that I ached for her ghost, that I worried she was alone and lost. I thought of the other babies leaving the hospital and the children they will grow into. They could have been Hannah's playmates, all of them turning somersaults and laughing under the trees. But they wouldn't want to play with her. They'd have no use for her ghost.

Before we left that room the cries of newborns came to us from down the hall. Amy lay still in bed, curled on her side and slipping in and out of sleep. I stared out into the fresh snow that had fallen and wiped out the previous day's bit of spring. The snow clung to the cottonwoods, and for the first time in my life I thought about how it would be to kill myself. It wasn't that I wanted to be with Hannah, that I thought I could somehow go to her or hold her, but that I would at least be *like* her. I wanted to be dead to be the same as Hannah.

I wouldn't do it though. Of course I wouldn't do it. I loved Amy now more than I ever had. I would stay with her and hold her and wait for days I knew would come when I would want to be alive.

But still I keep picturing that foot emerging from my wife, that minute, purple, translucent, perfect foot that made it suddenly, shockingly clear to me that this was real.

When Amy was discharged I wheeled her down to the hospital entrance and left her there while I went to get the truck. When I returned and saw her small and sunk down in the wheelchair in front of those doors that slid open for the people coming and going around her, she looked completely alone and exhausted. She had her elbow on the chair arm and her chin propped up on her palm. As if her head were too heavy to hold up otherwise. She looked blankly off toward the houses beyond the parking lot.

I got out and opened the door for her. She got in and patted Yukon on the head. "Hello boy," she said. "Let's get out of here."

A couple hours after we came home, the sun broke out again—the latest chapter in the unfolding struggle between winter and spring. Amy slept more and I walked up to Carlson's Field with Yukon. He'd gone into town with us the day of Amy's ultrasound, before we knew she'd wind up in the hospital and we'd be there for four days. Except for a walk every few hours, he'd been in the pickup in the hospital parking lot the entire time, and now walking up the cabin road, he was giddy, bounding through the melting snow and rolling in it, kicking his absurdly big paws in the air.

I hiked up to the spot where we think Hannah was probably conceived. The ground was still a couple feet down under snow, but a few tufts of the tallest shafts of hay grass showed through and bobbed in the wind that rode along the snow's surface.

I took off all my clothes and paced a circle in the snow. I was amazed at how far off the icy pain on the bottom of my feet was, at how insulated I felt from the wind that moved near my skin. I put my clothes back on and pulled up my heavy pack boots and sat down and stared at the snow between my knees.

I looked up toward the trees at the edge of the field in every direction and the valley and mountains beyond. When the sun had dropped into the dark row of white fir behind me, I saw that, on the now slate-blue surface of the snow, my disappeared shadow was indistinguishable from the shadow not cast by my daughter.

I left before the sky darkened deeper, before night could find us up there.

Today, Amy packed up Hannah's clothes—the OshKosh railroad overalls, the red fleece jumper with white polar bears. Quickly, and without faltering, she put the clothes in a box with the oversize books and teething ring and big plastic keys. She packed up all of this and the yellow rubber ducky and found a marker and wrote on the box BABY THINGS.

The things of this world are still the things of this world. The only difference is Hannah will never see or hold them. Walking the aisles of Safeway, looking for medicine and high-iron foods—broccoli and asparagus—for Amy's recovery, I saw wine bottles, bagels, shopping cart wheels, and faces, and all of it, every single thing, was another thing Hannah would never know.

The world when Amy was pregnant seemed a world waiting for its full truth, a world only half created, waiting to be filled by our child's perceptions. Other children will be born, maybe even Hannah's siblings to come, but the world will never be what it could have been through Hannah's eyes.

I put on my empty backpack, and Amy and I set out for the cabin. In four days we'll be going back to northern Michigan, to Marquette, her hometown, and we needed to retrieve a few books and clothes for the trip. We walked down the road from my uncle's place and past my grandparents' old ranch house, where smoke from the evening fire was drifting up from the chimney into a slate sky. At the machine shed we turned and started up the steep climb to the cabin.

The hill road was thigh deep with snow so we stopped every few minutes for Amy to catch her breath. She is getting better physically. Her shuffle is gone and she's started walking with her back straighter, her shoulders not rolled so far forward. And, despite my objections, she had insisted on coming. As we stood there, huffing clouds of breath and looking back over the valley that was falling away beneath and behind us, I found myself ready for us to get out of Idaho for a while. I feel as though Amy will survive her grief if we can just get her home to Marquette, to the streets of her childhood—those woods, movie theaters, and restaurants filled with the comforting familiarity of her past.

There will be Lake Superior. That biggest freshwater lake in the world. Amy's known its sound since her own infancy, and if the flat cover of ice has broken up or drifted off toward Canada when we arrive, she'll be able to hear the cold waves in the wind as we lie in bed across town. I have imagined those waves might speak to her with our daughter's voice.

And in Marquette will be Amy's own family. My family here—Steve, Marguerite, my cousins and grandparents—have been quiet around us, speaking in hushed tones about neutral things, giving us room. But what Amy needs now is not more calmness, more repose. What she needs now is not my family and not Idaho. She needs that primal embrace only her own mother can give her. Her mother, with whom she can, I'm hoping, open completely and weep without stopping herself.

I am worried about her, and getting her home is the one

thing I know to do. She's so often steady, so seemingly balanced, like she was when she told me she wanted to go with me up to the cabin. "It'll be good to get outside," she'd said this morning.

But this afternoon, getting dressed after a shower at Steve's house, she called out to me. I came in to the bedroom and found her sitting on the edge of the bed, looking down at her swollen breasts. To reduce the swelling she's been holding ice packs on them several times a day for the three days she's been home from the hospital. She's even spread cabbage on them in accordance with one of the nurses' suggestions, trying to get her breasts to realize they are not needed despite this recent birth, that they should sink against Amy's ribs again and wait.

But there, after her warm shower, a single drop of milk had formed on the end of one nipple. Tears streaked her cheeks and she looked up at me. "I thought it was over," she sobbed. "Now this."

"My belly is so hollow," she said, her voice quiet then as I held her. "I wish they could put her back inside me and I could make her better."

It was frightening to see her so shattered, but I was more frightened by her steady eyes when she looked up at me after catching her breath on the hill below the cabin and said, "Okay. Let's go on. I'm fine."

Maybe in Marquette she will be able to let her sorrow run loose. Maybe.

I must remember to stay close. I reminded myself of this as we trudged through the snow. I must remember to keep watch.

The cabin was cold and empty. The daffodils in the plastic mug on the windowsill were still in full bloom two weeks after I'd given them to Amy. The recent freezing and thawing temperatures apparently had been ideal for keeping them alive.

"Let's leave them here," I suggested.

"Yes. The place ought to have a touch of color, of life," Amy said.

I thought how, if some small spirit should pass through this otherwise abandoned home while we are gone, those bowed yellow heads might be some version of company.

We stood at the shelf and each of us pulled down a few books and then shuffled through our stack of CDs. These we stuffed down into my backpack; then we climbed the narrow stairs to the loft and went through the steamer trunk for clothes—underwear, socks, T-shirts, jeans, flannel shirts. We stacked them folded on the bed as we have for so many trips before, then packed them in the backpack too.

When I clicked closed the cabin door behind us, the sky was darker. The day was about over, and it occurred to me that it was Wednesday and Hannah has been cremated for two days.

I have always believed my life was my own. Not simply in the sense that I could quit a job or declare my love for someone, but I've always believed that my very experience emanated from some magical marriage between the world and my own will. If I really, really focused on Amy making it home through the blizzard, I knew I'd see her headlights soon, coming up the road. And, sure enough, there she'd be, every time. If I pictured our life, Amy's and Hannah's and mine together in the sunshine and cut-hay smell of a late summer afternoon, I'd be in that vision come September, natural and inevitable, certain as my hand holding this pen. I believed I was writing a life for us to live. Now, nine months before my thirtieth birthday, my beautiful illusion had dissolved and the world had been revealed distant and indifferent.

Near the cabin, in a tall stack of building scraps the snow had melted enough to reveal, I found a foot-long piece of larch pole that we had cut off one of the wall logs.

I had been hoping to find a short length of log like this to hollow out for Hannah's urn—a piece of our house, her house, in which to carry her back to Marquette. I stuffed it down into the pack, pulled the drawstring closed around the top again, and lifted the strap back to my shoulder.

Amy didn't ask me what the piece of wood was for. She was somewhere far off inside herself, and neither of us spoke on the way back down.

For the first time in my life I had arrangements in that sense of the word that means those things you have to do when someone dies. I rented a car down in Spokane yesterday for the drive back to Marquette. I finished Hannah's urn last night, wood shavings accumulating around my feet as I hollowed out a bowl shape in the end of the short piece of log from our cabin. When I was done, it was a crude job, something that looked like a first-year, high school wood-shop project.

I carved and carved but the wood was wet from sitting in the snow all winter. Instead of cutting smooth and dry, the log seeped gold water when I pressed the knife into it. And I was tired from the long drive from Spokane, my hands clumsy and thick. Despite sanding until my fingers were raw, the bottom and sides of the bowl were still rough, almost fuzzy with wood fibers.

"It's exactly how I want it," Amy said when I showed her my work.

"I wish I was a skilled woodcarver," I said.

"Don't say that." She rubbed her fingers around the lip of the urn. "It should be natural, how it was as a tree."

Amy had her own arrangements to make at work. In the morning she went in to prepare the shelter staff for her absence.

They have four clients, the most they've had in two months of operation. Four battered women. All this late-season fluctuation between fresh snow and melt is pushing people to the brink. There is violence behind people's eyes in the grocery store and post office in Sandpoint, and even out here at the Westmond General Store. It's good that the sun is out today. And it is good that we are leaving northern Idaho for a couple of weeks.

After dropping Amy at the shelter, I went by the funeral home to pick up Hannah's ashes. The young man there handed me a little envelope, the extra small kind where you have to fold the paper up and fold it again on one side to make your letter fit.

"That's her?" I asked.

The funeral home man set the envelope on his desk beside some papers for me to sign. "That's her. I'm so sorry," he said as I lifted the ashes. "This is hard."

"Yes," I said back to him, feeling how light the ashes were in my hand, "hard."

I signed where the papers were highlighted in yellow.

The funeral home doesn't charge to cremate babies, so I was done and free to leave with the envelope.

"Thank you."

"Give my condolences to your wife," he said and stood as I stood to leave. He offered me his hand. "Let us know if we can do anything else."

"Thank you," I said again, accepting the handshake and really noticing him for the first time since I'd walked in, his brow furled in an earnest expression under his thick dark hair. He was younger than I am.

I sat the envelope in the urn in the back seat of the rental Pontiac and drove out of town, up toward the Canada line, passing the occasional log truck along the otherwise deserted highway. The sky was razor bright, and the deep snowpacks of the Selkirk Mountains rose around the car, fresh snow weighing down pine boughs and barn roofs.

I had Willie Nelson on the tape deck. His voice came bright and clean through those speakers, and I turned it up until I couldn't hear any of my own thoughts over his words.

I was fine, driving eighty on a dry, sunbaked road, the ashes silent in the urn in the back seat. I was fine. Until the first few lines of "Angel Flyin' too Close to the Ground" brought an overwhelming wave of sadness. All the selflessness of fatherhood that my life had been moving toward had evaporated, and I was back in my skin, in this self-indulgent drive into the sun-bleached, snowy mountains alone.

Hannah was the other, the one who was to have pulled me out of myself. With her gone I will have to work to stay connected to this world. I know Amy will need me like never before, and I am making a deliberate effort to hold on.

But speeding along Highway 95, I could feel the Canada line up ahead, the give of that new accelerator pedal under my foot as I pushed down coming out of the curves and straightened that tight steering wheel. The low, near sides of mountains blurred. Summit crests above the canyon moved toward and past me like crests of waves. Willie sang loud his song of a fallen angel, and I wept, and Hannah was Hannah in her envelope in the hollowed-out log in the back seat as that seafoam-green Pontiac sailed us toward what might as well have been the edge of the earth.

At Amy's follow-up appointment at the Sandpoint Women's Health Clinic, Dr. Bowden gave us the okay to travel back to Marquette. Sheepishly we told her we'd already rented a car for the trip. "We're a little on the willful side," Amy admitted.

Bowden listened to us tell of the crushing grief we'd been through the last week, and she reassured us when we asked about future babies that, "Yes, there's every reason to hope Amy's next pregnancy will be successful. The key will be getting a stitch around that cervix early in the second trimester."

Next pregnancy. The words sounded to my ear like blasphemy. I knew though that they wouldn't always, and I was glad there would be something that could be done to keep this from happening again.

Before we left we asked if she'd want to step out of character and have dinner with us when we got back.

She brightened. "I'd really love to," she said. "And, I'd love for you to meet Steve. He's heard a lot about you guys, anonymously of course. I really leaned on him last week when this was happening."

Friends. It looked as though we might end up making bright, worldly, compassionate friends out of this. Pain can draw people together, can strip away pretense and leave the kind core of empathy, as we sit together in the truths of our fragile, precious lives.

May it be so with Amy and me, I thought to myself. May we find and hold each other through this suffering.

If your wife dies, you are a widower. If your parents die, you are an orphan. I know of no word for what you become when death leaves you childless. There should be a word.

We crossed the Montana line, heading east out of Idaho toward Michigan. Amy slept while I drove, then just north of Missoula I looked over at her and she was awake, her eyes were wide and filled with tears, and she'd been watching me. I held her hand and cried silently with her as the car moved down through its long turns into that gray valley. At the edge of the city, we passed a small herd of elk grazing on the steep earth-cut above the highway. They will have begun their migration back up into the high country by the time we pass through there again in April.

We're back in that other hometown, Marquette, Michigan. A couple days after we got here, Amy and I drove up to Big Bay, a little lumber town a half-hour north of Marquette. The Big Bay Road winds along Lake Superior and through the low Huron Mountains. On one side tens of thousands of acres of hemlock and white pine and birch give shelter to moose and black bears and a healthy number of timber wolves; on the other side the lake widens like a flat desert of ice falling over the horizon toward the Arctic.

Because it is frozen over, we won't be able to spread Hannah's ashes in the water this winter, which is just as well. We aren't ready to let them go.

I don't know where to turn now that landscape is not enough to sustain me. If any place could call me back to the goodness of life, the Big Bay Road could. Instead, Amy and I fought.

Amy told me that she is deeply angry, enraged at herself and me—angry at herself because she kept working, which she believes could well be the reason Hannah is dead, angry at me because I was very much in favor of her working so I could keep writing and building the cabin.

I reminded her that Dr. Bowden had said she could keep working, and I insisted this terrible thing hadn't been anyone's fault. "I admit I wanted to keep writing, but God, if I'd known, if I thought that you would lose the baby because you were working . . . I didn't want to believe it."

"I don't care. My baby is dead and I never get another chance. I was supposed to be her mother, her *mother*, and I didn't take care of her because I was working."

"I looked for work. At the Forest Service and with that log home builder. We only had a few weeks," I said quietly, but I knew I had been greedy, jealously guarding my writing time and the life we had in the cabin as I assured her everything would be all right.

Amy just watched the woods slip by. I'd never seen her so inconsolable. I was frightened to feel so far from the one person who shared this grief with me, frightened that I would wind up alone after all this. Beyond that, I was frightened that I might believe what she was saying, that it was our fault, this thing that had happened to us.

"And I'm mad at you because I didn't feel like you were there emotionally when I came home from the hospital," she added finally.

I wanted to jump out of the car and run into the woods or into the lake and disappear.

"Jesus Christ, I was out of my mind then. I could hardly speak."

"I know it. But you weren't there to listen to me. You were so upset."

"I never left your side," I insisted, though I knew that she wasn't talking about a physical absence.

The world seemed foreign. I didn't recognize the trees along the road. My own hands on the wheel. Where were we going? Amy had already told me she was having a difficult time thinking about returning to the cabin with no running water and lumber stacked everywhere and no fridge or kitchen stove. "I just want to have a normal, settled life," she'd said. Now she was telling me that at her most desperate time I'd failed to provide the economic and emotional support she needed.

She looked very much alone, staring out the window, her hands together in her lap.

We turned around in Big Bay, in the parking lot of the General Store with the plastic moose on the roof, Christmas lights still strung in his antlers. We didn't stop into the Big Bay Hotel restaurant for a bowl of whitefish chowder as I thought we might. We didn't go into the Lumberjack Bar for a quick drink. We headed back onto the highway toward Marquette in silence.

"I'm sorry," I said after several minutes. "I wanted so bad to pull myself together for you last week. I want to finish the cabin for you, to make it comfortable. I wish to hell I'd found a job and hadn't clung to my precious writing time like a spoiled kid."

"You were wonderful," she sobbed and grabbed hold of my arm up near my shoulder. "You never left me in the hospital, and all the women at the shelter are jealous of how kind you are and of our relationship. Oh, I'm just so fucking mad! I never sang to her or rocked her or was alone with her." Amy was clutching my arm harder now, crying into my shoulder. I pulled off the road and we held each other in the idling car and wept.

"What am I supposed to do with all the baby clothes?" she cried. "The toys and the books? What will I do with my maternity clothes? I don't want to have more children. I want my baby. I wanted to ask Dr. Bowden to take my incompetent cervix and cut it up into a thousand pieces. That way I'll never let another baby down."

The air was quiet in the wake of her rage.

"We don't get another chance," she said finally and sighed a deep, deep sigh. "I just want her back."

I am determined that our marriage will hold together. It must. But what are we holding on for? What is left of our lives?

Each other. That is the answer, of course. But how we keep each other in sight as we wander so far into the blackness of our individual griefs, I don't know.

We sat there for a moment longer.

"God, how will I function at work?" Amy said, rubbing her eyes.

"You really want to go back?" I asked, pulling the car onto the road again.

"The shelter is a way out of how I feel. It's the only thing I can imagine that will keep me from sinking forever into this," she answered.

"For me it's the same with the cabin," I said. "I need to finish that place, to feel the wood in my fists, to make it happen."

"We'll go back," she said. "We've got to live someplace. But I am fed up with exposed insulation and midnight outhouse trips."

"I'll work faster, stay focused," I assured her.

"I'm not saying that. I'm just so damn tired of struggling."

"I know. Me too," I said. "It's good we're here for a while." The highway hummed under us. "Marquette and our families can't save us, but at least they can help us endure. For a few weeks, anyway."

"I guess, yeah. I'm glad we came," Amy said.

A dozen miles outside Marquette, we turned from the Big Bay Road onto a plowed two-track where people have been feeding corn and hay and rotten lettuce to whitetail deer.

We got out and stood with our arms around each other beside that aqua-colored rental car covered with the dried mud and road salts of the northern United States. I rubbed her back. The fleece of her coat was soft under my hands.

"People ask me how I'm doing," Amy said. "Do they want to know the truth?"

"Some of them," I said.

The deer, maybe a hundred in among the woods, only glanced up and went back to their food, less afraid of us than of the burning hunger in their guts.

"They're thin," Amy said.

"Yes. If the snow gets too much deeper they'll be in trouble."

"I hope they make it to spring."

"They're almost there."

In our grief and exhaustion we've grown passive, giving ourselves over to our families and to Marquette. And it would be easy to just stay. Old friends have started to call to get together. Amy's folks take us cross-country skiing and out to dinner. When we can't sleep, my folks stay up late and keep us company while we watch the local TV news.

Some nights, when Amy does sleep, I walk.

I walk the neighborhoods of my high school and college years, past bars I know too well, past the King Koin laundromat on Third Street, the smell of moist, warm, lint steam drifting down from the roof exhaust. The streets of town have narrowed with snow that tumbles back down the high banks after plows pass, their six-foot-tall blades not high enough to toss all the fresh powder clear. Walking Marquette is like navigating a maze of trenches, the branches of oak trees and gables of houses above, on the new, elevated surface of the world.

When I return to whichever of our parents' houses we're staying at that night, I stand outside for a while, across the street. It's comfortable to stand there in the cold, perfectly still air and know that Amy is inside, warm and asleep. The windows are all dark, including the one behind which she is sleeping. It looks like all the other dark windows in town, and it seems such a small space when I think that behind it is so much of what I call my life.

I sat in the Marquette Village Pub on Third Street at one in the morning with my friend Mac, both of us drunk. I hadn't had a drink since Amy's pregnancy was first diagnosed as risky, but I wanted to drink with Mac. He told me everything about his son's death six weeks before. He showed me Shaun's new driver's license and told me how it'd been covered in blood. He told me about sitting in his office at the University Counseling Center, listening to troubled students, trying to focus on their pain and their self-doubts while his own grief stormed inside him.

Mac goes to the cemetery every day. He is buying up grave plots around Shaun for himself and his other kids. He had Shaun's fleece jacket professionally cleaned of blood and flesh for Shaun's younger brother to wear.

"I didn't want to wash out all the body stuff, didn't want to clean off the license, to wipe off the blood. It's real, I need that. I love that," he said, staring into his beer.

He held his head up with his hand at his temple. His fingers were ashen and wrinkled, like bark. Older than mine. And the straight black hair that leaked like water between his fingers was streaked with gray.

Mac honks his horn when he passes the spot of the accident. Someone has inscribed a cross with the words "God Bless You Boys" in big black letters and driven the cross into the top of the ten-foot snowbank beside the road. The entire town is mourning.

When I told him that I feel distant from what he must feel, unraveling his heart from the daily threads of Shaun's presence, Mac lifted his eyes to mine. Deep in their wrinkled, freckled folds of skin those eyes were kind and knowing and unspeakably sad when he answered, "But Shaun got to live. Shaun got sixteen years. One of his friends, a beautiful girl a year older than him, was teaching him to kiss. Hannah won't have that."

I didn't want my loss to be in league with the black hole of Mac's, and it *is* different. But Mac was right. Hannah has been robbed of all of it, of the touch of her face by some high school kid's hand as he leans in to kiss her. And for me, just as for Mac, any future I thought I had a hold of, any sense of owning this life beyond the present moment, was gone.

Earlier that day, eating breakfast at my parents' dining room table, watching children at recess at the school across the street, I was overwhelmed by hopelessness. I thought of how, only a couple weeks before, my father must have sat at that same table watching those same kids climb and tumble down that giant snowbank and thought, with the deepest satisfaction, how his own grandchild would be among them.

Walking home from the closed bar in the falling snow, through the deserted town under the blinking stoplights, I loved Mac with a compassion and understanding I'd never felt toward any friend before. I've had close friends all my life, people whose stories I weave gratefully into my own. Now though, stopping to watch those stoplights pulse yellow and red, back and forth, lighting up the snow in the air with yellow and red light, I knew I'd crossed over into some new level of human connection.

Mac spoke of a fence between the living and the dead that he now gazes across daily. I think there is also a fence between those, the grieving, who can see into that furthest region and those who cannot. I have Hannah to thank for much of who I become from now on, for leading me here. If not for Hannah, I would never have had the honor of hearing Mac describe how, when he got to the hospital, the nurses had laid out Shaun's body on a bed in a normal hospital room, how he held his son and stroked his hair and drank in, for the last time, his musky, adolescent smell. If not for Hannah, Mac could not have told me how, despite having been killed by a combined collision speed of a hundred miles an hour, Shaun had looked worse with bad cases of childhood flu and tooth-breaking falls off his bicycle. If not for my own daughter and her death, Mac would not have been able to tell me how the only thing wrong with his son that night in the hospital was that he kept growing colder. Because of Hannah, I knew exactly what he meant.

We had Hannah's memorial service in a low, tiny chapel in Marquette. Greg—one of my closest friends and the preacher who married Amy and me in the June sunshine on a cliff top above Lake Superior two and a half years ago—presided over this other rite. My parents and sister, Amy's parents and sister, Amy's sister's boyfriend, Greg's wife and oldest daughter—all of us pressed broken glass chips and tiles into mortar, creating a big mosaic for Amy and me, and a pair of smaller mosaics, one for each pair of our parents. The collective, abstract grief made tangible in fragments.

We sang songs. We wept bitterly. I held Amy under the crook of my arm. On the altar in front of us, the candle Amy'd lit at the start of the service burned beside the log urn. On the top of the urn, in the little bowl-like depression, wrapped in a linen cloth tied with a purple bow, were the ashes to which we sang and spoke and wept.

When everyone had said their consoling words about how we were together in our familial love because of Hannah, and how Hannah was in God's presence, how she'd changed us all forever and brought us together, Amy spoke up.

"I'm glad that you all can be comforted," she started in a voice that seemed to come from far off, barely audible in the absolute stillness. "I really am. But I just want her here. She would have brought us together alive. She would be here now. I'm sorry, but I never got to sing to her and rock her and hold her hand. Not as a living baby."

In the wake of Amy's pronouncement we all sat, concurring in silence. Then I read from Wordsworth's "Ode: Intimations on Immortality from Recollections of Early Childhood," section IX, which ends:

> *Hence in a season of calm weather*
> *Though inland far we be,*
> *Our Souls have sight of that immortal sea*
> *Which brought us hither,*
> *Can in a moment travel thither,*
> *And see the Children sport upon the shore,*
> *And hear the mighty waters rolling evermore.*

Soon Amy and I would be going to our own inland, back from this frozen freshwater sea to the mountains.

But I still wasn't sure we should go. Our parents and Marquette had been good for us. The morning after the service, we drove the back roads thirty miles east of town with Amy's dad—his elbow and mine out the open windows of his big, new pickup and Amy on the seat between us. Amy's dad was quiet behind his aviator's sunglasses and gray mustache. He's a stoic man, steady and solid, and I was glad to have him there, glad to be sharing the job of keeping Amy company with him.

We saw a hunting bald eagle and, minutes later, a hunting red-tailed hawk. Amy's dad said that, in the bright sunlight and fifty-degree temperatures, the hunting must have been ideal, with field mice and squirrels and rabbits out enjoying the first warmth of spring.

Now, the last day before we leave, spring seems to widen with the open sky, and the snow continues to run as clear melt-water down the dirty gutters and off the multigabled roofs of the big, old, lumber-town houses. College kids on mountain bikes jump off curbs and zip between cars, showing off their newly bared legs, and the first canvas Jeep tops are rolled back, and there is blue water visible way out beyond the pack ice on Superior.

Leaving Marquette is always tough. But this time, even though we're going back to the cabin that's been my dream since I can remember and the landscape I loved first and purest as a child, leaving here, where Amy is surrounded by her own family and place, seems like a dangerous move. I am worried about us both, about our sense of hope and our faith in the goodness of the world. Afraid of what returning to Idaho and relying so completely on each other as we grieve will mean for us. I see glimpses of renewal here in this bright sunlight, and I am afraid to leave.

The Third
Trimester

The car that brought you here still runs.

— Richard Hugo

When we returned to Idaho enough snow had melted that the steep road to the cabin, the hill road, was passable. I'd been worried that we'd be filled with dread at seeing the place, or more honestly, I'd worried that Amy would be. I'd worried that the fresh memories of struggle and loss would turn her against our little home. But when we topped the hill and saw that green metal roof shining in the sun, she grabbed my arm and said, "There it is!"

She was out of the truck before I had it turned off, walking between patches of snow, talking about the deck we planned to build and where she wanted to plant flowers. "Right here in front of where the deck will end," she said, hands on her hips, surveying the ground around her. "A row of them where they'll get sunlight all day, and a circle of flowers around this big boulder."

She paused and looked up at the cabin. "I'm sure I'll be frustrated by it all, the difficulties of it here, many more times," she said. "But right now I'm thinking how this is the one time in our lives we'll be building this home."

It's not that we were kidding ourselves. Hannah still haunted us. After we swept and shook out the sheets and rugs and unpacked, we sat quietly paying bills, both of us stealing glances up at her ashes on the top of the bookcase where we'd put them, still wrapped in white linen and tied with a purple bow, still atop the log urn. Our daughter's ashes will be there for a long time, until August when we go back to spread them in Lake Superior.

But we've returned to sunshine and longer evenings, a new bull calf born while we were away, and robins hopping around on the spots of bare ground. All of it has to mean our side of the earth is tilting back toward the sun.

Idaho doesn't hear prayers. No place does. But I'm hoping Idaho will help make me new again. Only this time it's Idaho's indifference I need. I want a wilderness wild in its disregard for Amy and me, a landscape bigger than our grief. The mountains, pines, birds, and bare-knuckled branches of aspen didn't refuse us our child. They didn't steal her back into themselves beyond the horizon ridge or into the night. Idaho has no targets, no malice or master plan. If we are to heal ourselves and hold on to each other, we will have to learn the lesson that this world had nothing to do with hurting us.

What I want out of being back here is to salvage our dream of a life in the woods and hold fast to our marriage. I don't know if that can be done when we've lost something so much more, a daughter. But I do know that daughter's legacy is entirely up to us; she's lost her ability to act on her own. And I refuse to allow her legacy to be parents who abandon themselves and each other to grief.

Our second afternoon back, when Amy was gone for her first shift at the shelter again, I discovered the little creek of water under our cabin was back, flowing out from the front of our foundation as it had during the horrible melt of New Year's. Now though, with the drifts around the cabin so much smaller, I could get around behind the back wall to see where the water was coming from. The sixty-degree day had been melting the remaining snowpack up in the alfalfa field faster than the water could soak into the ground, and the runoff was streaming down and pooling at our back wall, where it apparently was trickling in under the house and through our foundation.

I spent two hours with a shovel and garden hoe, digging a trench around the side of the cabin. I dug off the snow first, then carved the channel into the icy mud. Each pull on the hoe opened the ground another few inches and the water streamed in. The work hurt. I've let my body get flabby the last few weeks—keeping vigil at the hospital for days, driving across the country to Marquette, then turning around and crossing the country again—and my back tightened and burned as I tossed mud and rocks to the side, between the new course of the stream and the cabin. I ran the trench along under the eave of the roof, where rainwater would fall, about three feet out from the wall. As more and more water followed my course, the pool at the back of the cabin started to drain.

I was pleased with myself to see it working, to see my channel fill with water and see the creek coming out the front of our foundation dry up. Indifference. Water doesn't care where it goes. The trick to diverting water, I discovered, is just to give it the idea of a new course, to get a little rivulet started where you want it all to eventually go and let time do most of the work for you.

As I stood leaning on the handle of the hoe and watching him, Yukon played with the new little stream, sniffing and pawing at it, then tossing his shaggy, white head in the air, lifting his big front paws up then slamming them down in the cold water—a miniature version of a polar bear fishing a river. The sun behind him was low in the trees but still burned gold on the face of Butler Mountain across the valley. That same sun was setting on thousands of square miles of mountains, mountains to the horizon, mountains in Canada and Montana, and mountains surrounding the cabin.

Through the dusk my cousin Heidi and her friend came up the road on their horses. They were two young college women home for spring break and beautiful on their huge, blond Norwegian Fjords, Chico and Chiquita. The horses hadn't been ridden in six months, and they stomped and snorted under the girls.

When the horses were tied off we went inside and talked and drank sodas that I'd had cooling in the dwindling cabin-side snowbank all day. I lit a fire in the stove and told them about diverting the runoff water around the cabin, and they told me about midterms and dorm life and guys.

When their sodas were empty and the girls had mounted back up and ridden off and left me and my place quiet again, I thought of the day, not of any specific thing I did, but of the day itself, how it had moved forward and how I had found its flow. I was crossing new ground, carving a new channel, and this was only one day.

April 8th, one month since Hannah was born and died, I spent the day fixing fence down by Westmond Creek, which rushed past full of meltwater. The work was meditative in its repetitiveness—stretching old wire, clipping sections of new wire and twisting it onto sections of the old, looking up at a quarter-mile of fence to go. The mountain air was clear and warm and chickadees darted between the still-bare cottonwoods. A coyote yipped somewhere in the valley, prompting a neighbor's dog to bark back. The cows wandered down and watched me for a while.

In the early evening Amy pulled up the dirt road on her way home from work, got out of the truck, and walked across the damp, new grass in her denim shirt and jeans. I was awed by how beautiful she was right then, how absolutely and mag-

nificently beautiful. Amy's a small woman, even girlish looking sometimes, with her river moss green eyes and dark hair
to her shoulders, but walking along the other side of that fence
toward me, coming home after a day in the trenches with battered wives and children, she was unmistakably a fiercely
strong woman.

I picked my tool belt up off the ground and threw it over my
shoulder. Like a saddle.

"Howdy," I called and grinned over the now piano wire–
taut top strand of barbed wire as I walked down to meet her.
"I'm your Marlboro Man."

"You don't smoke," she said and gave me a kiss before pulling me in for a tight, long embrace.

"You smell like sunshine," she said and I realized that silly little moment was the first spot of pure, unequivocal happi-
ness we've shared since before Amy went into the hospital.

Man's Body Discovered in Cabin the headline says. A snowmobil-
er found a man dead in a cabin in the high country a few miles
north of here. He had been up there all winter, trapped. I've
cut out the article and pinned it to the window frame above
the wash basin. I can imagine the way he dreamed at night of
people he loved, of his wife's hair, if he had a wife. The lives we
live are not myths; they are our lives. If any of us are ever saved,
whatever that might mean, we aren't saved by the stories we
create for ourselves to inhabit; we are saved by our loves.

Amy, her friend Deb, and I sat at a long table eating homemade
enchiladas, then cheesecake, then drinking beer as the slow,
wide, green Clark Fork moved by outside the window of Deb's

house. Deb was good company for us. She's Amy's coworker from the shelter, and through those long weeks when Amy had to work lying on her back, it was Deb who ran the errands to the grocery store and courthouse, who sprang up to answer the buzz at the door intercom so Amy wouldn't have to get out of her deck chair. And time and again as Amy and I fretted and complained, Deb listened sympathetically, as she was listening now over the enormous dinner she'd cooked for us.

We talked about how we've lost our sense of the future, how we don't know what will become of us now that our dream of raising this baby has dissolved.

"I don't know how you'll recover," Deb said, shaking her head as if at the supreme incomprehensibility of our loss. "But you will. You'll never be over it, probably. You shouldn't be. But you'll have lives you care about again. It doesn't feel like it, I know."

As comforting as it was to hear the kindness in her voice and the pain she felt for us, it wasn't her words that gave me reason to hope. It was her example. Deb is ten years older than Amy and me, and she's single. She moved up here years ago with a husband, who promptly left her once their dream of escaping Los Angeles for the wilderness was a reality. But she's stayed. She's stayed and learned the high country where the sweetest huckleberries ripen in September. She's driven her old Toyota Land Cruiser over every mile of logging road on the Green Monarch Mountain Ridge, and she's joined a tiny church that holds barn dances, and she found the job at the shelter working with Amy.

With her house on the river and her four dogs and an enduring compassion that draws her to work with abused women and sit up late into the night talking with her grief-stricken friends, Deb knows perseverance. And spending time in her presence helps me imagine Amy and I might persevere, too.

Hours after we'd come home from Deb's and gone to bed and fallen asleep, Amy woke in the dark. I don't know how long she'd been crying when she spoke my name and woke me up. She didn't have anything new to say, just that she was terribly guilty.

"I was so selfish when I was pregnant," she said. "I wanted to keep everything how it was, the cabin, my job. I didn't want to lose my independence."

"You didn't know. Everyone feels like that I would guess. But they get beyond it because the baby comes."

"And now I feel guilty over everything. I don't feel like I should be laughing or having dinner with Deb. I'm working at the shelter like Hannah never existed, throwing myself into it."

"I know," I said, thinking how I have to just keep listening. Listening and holding her when she reaches for me, which is what I did. I held her as her river of grief flowed on and the mountains soared around us in the night.

I'd finished building a morning fire and was warming my palms in front of the woodstove glass when Amy called down to me from the loft. She called me casually, like she wanted her slippers, or another blanket thrown over her. When I sat down beside her on the bed, she reached up and kissed me. We made love for the first time in months.

After, we stayed in bed until noon, snoozing off and on and listening to the rain on the metal roof.

"I don't talk to her as much as I used to," Amy finally said, looking up at me from where her head had been resting on my chest. "I used to say good-night to her every night and talk to her sometimes when I'd be driving to work, even after she was gone. Now, I go two or three days without saying anything." She was quiet for a while then said, "I often think I can feel her kick."

Amy rested her head back down on my chest. I stared up at the pine boards I'd nailed to the ceiling the day before. Those boards are so smooth, so clear and bright with grain that swirls and parts for knots and comes back together like spring creek water moving around rocks. New wood looks like hope.

Carlson's Field is for sale. Billy, the guy who bought it from Carlson's son for sixty thousand then logged the forest ringing the field for probably thirty thousand dollars in timber, this same guy now wants a *hundred* and sixty thousand dollars for the property. He'd sell it off in parcels, I'm certain, but I've heard the neighbor who granted him easement for a road stipulated it was for one dwelling only.

Amy and I certainly don't have $160,000, nor do any of my family members in Idaho.

I won't walk up there for a while. Any solace I might find would be short-circuited by visions of the inevitable house that will squat on that hill and the long, gravel driveway that will be cut like a wound through the grass.

Amy's twenty-eighth birthday was a few days ago. She's always wanted a rocking chair, the kind with the big, wide, flat armrests—like the one at her family's log cabin in Michigan—a chair in which she could sit in front of the fire and lean back and hear that familiar creaking, always at the same spot in the rocking motion. After looking in antique stores for such a rocker for months, I found one the day before her birthday.

I brought it home before Amy returned from work and tied a big purple ribbon around it.

When she walked through the door, she stopped and shouted my name and threw her arms around me. She sat down. She rocked back. She stood up and sat down again. She scooted the chair and a footstool over by the woodstove and pretended to warm her feet there, though it was a warm, sunny day and last night's fire was long out.

She stood up and hugged me again, then digging herself in closer, started to sob against my chest. "Oh Buddy," she cried, "I feel like we shouldn't be celebrating."

Looking over at the rocker she said, "I imagined rocking Bean to sleep in a rocker just like that."

I am always startled to hear Hannah called Bean now, even when I say it myself. I couldn't think of anything to tell Amy, except, "Me too."

"I do love it though," she sighed finally, recovering from her flash of grief almost as quickly as she'd been hit by it. "I think I'm a little sad to be so far from home, too."

This was the first birthday in years that Amy hasn't been with her own family. Packages from Marquette came in the mail, and we went out for a big dinner and sat out on the deck at the restaurant in Sandpoint, washing down our burritos with margaritas, but we had to admit, we both missed the wild steelhead trout Amy's father traditionally fixes for her birthday.

My family here really came through, though. Two day's after Amy's birthday, we held our first party in the cabin. Uncles, aunts, and cousins came in from around northern Idaho and over in Washington. All of them, even my grandparents, packed into four-wheel-drives in the front yard of the old farmhouse and drove up the steep road to our cabin. I couldn't find steelhead, but Safeway did have Alaskan salmon on sale, so I grilled that up, and we threw a bag of ice in the cooler to chill the beer and wine.

Somehow we all squeezed into this little space. The smell of barbecuing fish and cool evening air drifted in through the open windows, and the sounds of our talking and laughter drifted out over the tree tops of Westmond Valley.

I served hot fudge ice cream cake, Amy's favorite dessert. We put candles on her serving and all sang "Happy Birthday," and Amy read her birthday cards out loud to everyone.

Otherwise on the shy side in crowds, she loves to bask in the attention of birthdays, loves the license they give her to be the center of things for a change. She tore open her gifts and hugged each giver, then tried on the sweatshirt, the hiking boots, put the new CD on the stereo.

Not long after dark, my grandmother whispered in my grandfather's ear, as she does when she's ready to call it a night, and soon everyone else climbed into their four-wheel-drives and headed down the road, back to the cluster of out-buildings and pair of houses at the front of the ranch, and on to homes elsewhere.

It wasn't a birthday in Marquette, but as she curled up in the rocking chair, Amy said it was certainly the next best thing. In a few minutes she was asleep, under a big fleece blanket her parents had sent, with her feet up on the footstool in front of a bright, energetic fire.

We danced last night. I was warming soup on the newly installed gas stove in our low kitchen. Amy was at the table figuring May's bills—how much for student loans and the truck payment, how much for the pine boards to finish the ceiling. Sandpoint radio was coming in clear, the signal bouncing its way up the valley and finding our old, dusty, battery-powered stereo, when they played Pure Prairie League's "Amy."

I'm a bad dancer anyway and was out of practice as we hadn't danced since early winter, but Amy helped me find the beat then let me lead, our shoes shuffling on the plywood floor, her dark, thick hair swaying across her shoulders and shining in the kerosene lamp light. Evening was ending in the first starlit blue behind the big triangle windows in the living room gable.

Later, Amy would lie awake beside me in the loft just above the kitchen where we danced. Later, she would talk about joining a group for grieving parents, about wanting to walk in the forest alone. Later, I would lie sleepless after Amy had at last drifted off, and I would picture Hannah's foot falling out into this world with a tiny, dead flop onto a hospital bed sheet.

But as we danced, all that suffering was later. "Amy, what you gonna do?" the radio sang as the smell of soup rose around us and we spun through that generous moment.

I heard the saw before I crested the hill. I hung back from the ridge where I could see the tops of the trees in the direction from which the noise was coming, but no one over there could see me.

Sure enough, the top of a Douglas fir started to quiver, then, as if in slow motion, topple, picking up speed as the branches flung back and the crackling sound finally reached me as the tree disappeared. Then I heard the whoosh of those branches that had only a moment before rushed through the air. I stared at the new gap in the row of trees, my eyes working over that absence like a tongue feeling its way over the gap where a yanked tooth had just been. At last the deep boom of the tree hitting the ground reached me and shook the earth under my feet like the shock wave of a distant bomb.

I crouched down right there, just short of the crest. When Billy bought Carlson's property a couple years ago, he logged the woods around the field hard. My grandfather said he saw the trucks coming out of the woods and turning onto the end of the gravel county road below his house, load after load of massive white pine, Doug fir, and larch every day.

Now, apparently, Billy was back for more, cashing in on the few big trees left before he sells the place for nearly three times what he paid for it.

I watched two more trees go. The saw revved on and I watched the tops, trying to guess which one was next, until I couldn't stand seeing the new gaps anymore and stood and turned and headed back down toward the cabin.

All the candles were blown out and we were almost ready to turn in. Then Amy asked me, as we sat in front of the fire for a few last minutes of evening, what I would do if she couldn't have kids.

How terrifying, to be a woman, terrifying in ways I've never dreamed of. "The question," I said very slowly after absorbing the magnitude of what she'd asked, "is 'what would *we* do?'"

"Yeah?"

"When I think of wanting a family, I only ever think of wanting one with you. I'm not being noble. I just never think of the possibility of kids with anyone else. We're it."

"That's good," Amy said. "I feel the same way."

And now that the subject was filling the air around us like the gold, quivering light from the woodstove window, she said, "How do you feel about another baby? Not right away.

Not yet. I'm not ready yet. I know you want to eventually. But how do you feel about soon? When we have insurance and everything?"

I knew by "everything" she meant, in part, once our sorrow over our first child had subsided enough to be distinguishable from our desire to be parents. But I knew also that by "soon" she meant months instead of years.

"It's Hannah I wanted," I said. "But if we can't have her, I want another."

"Me too," Amy said quickly. It was as if we'd had to surprise ourselves with those sentences. We'd been stalking them for weeks, neither of us quite knowing when they would show themselves through the tangle and undergrowth of talk.

"It feels disloyal," Amy said.

"It does," I agreed. "But that's only because we're not there yet."

I saw the elk. After six months of seeing only their tracks and scat and stalking them through these woods and listening to other people's accounts of them, I finally saw them. A cow and her calf. Or, more accurately, a cow and, just above the grass, the top of a little calf head with oversized ears. I walked up into Carlson's Field at dusk figuring Billy and his chainsaw would be gone by then. And there they were. Elk. Long after I'd have thought they'd be back up on Butler Mountain.

Fortunately, I'd left Yukon back at the cabin. I crouched down in the grass and crept forward. The wind was just right, coming at me straight from them, and I got to within fifty yards or so before being spotted. The mother's head lifted and turned toward me. A split second later her calf peered above the grass, and those two big calf ears pointed my way.

A mother and her young. I stared at them. They stared at me.

In that moment I was hit by the urge to shout Hannah's name to them. I wanted to do this not because of any ethereal, magical reason. It's not that I thought that they needed to know the name of a new ghost haunting these woods with them. I didn't believe that they could deliver my daughter's spirit to me or deliver my love to her.

No, I simply wanted the fact that Hannah had existed to have impact on the animal world. She was born, though dead, with a name. I wanted that name to vibrate in their ears, to shoot up their aural nerves and go off in an explosion of electricity in their brains. I wanted Hannah's name bursting inside those elk like a supernova as they bounded over fences and deadfall logs into the dark forest and out of sight.

But I couldn't do it. The elk looked up at me and their muscles went tense. I wanted them to stay. I wanted just another second. I wanted to memorize the dark brown swirls of fur on the cow's long, strong neck, wanted to memorize the silhouette of those calf elk ears piqued above the grass and silhouetted in the last light of dusk.

Thinking about it now, I also believe I didn't want to give up Hannah's name, as if calling it to these elk would release it, her name, her entire worldly estate, from the warm darkness of my own lungs.

In an instant they were over the barbed wire, not with the weightlessness of the whitetail deer that seem to barely touch ground when on the run, but with the explosion of horses jumping.

I stood up and stared into the thinned woods where they had gone. The field was empty around me.

Butler Mountain, our mountain, is named after a Forest Service ranger who was struck by lightning and killed somewhere on a high ridge up there years ago. The mountain keeps his name all the way down to its rocky core. Carlson died and (at least in my language of place) left his name across his field like the long, cursive shadows of wind that tilt the hay grass.

It was June 8th, three months since Hannah was born and died. Where in the world, what creature or landform, will have the name of an infant whose eyes never saw the light of day, whose only existence beyond a weightless, warm, language-less womb was in the expectations and affections of those of us who survive? To Hannah, her own name, if I had spoken it through cupped hands into Amy's swollen belly, would have been without meaning. It would have been as it would have been for the elk, a formless firing of neurons like fireflies rising in summer air, or a whole night sky of stars revealing themselves at once and only for a twinkling instant. This is what I had in my chest. This brightness is what I didn't want to speak and release.

I'd been working with my uncle Steve on a contract we received to build a house. We rolled in to the job site every morning at 7:30, fired up the generator, buckled our tool belts, and (except for an hour at lunch) measured, sawed, squared, and hammered until six in the evening. I enjoyed the rhythm of the work, the way it felt to hold the worn wood handle of a framing hammer in my hand, the heft of the steel head at the end. I liked the way it felt to toss my tool belt onto the truck seat beside me at the end of the day. I liked the way it felt to be earning money.

But when Steve and I showed up to work one morning, the homeowner, our boss, told us he wasn't happy with how it was going. He'd been following us around with a tape measure for days and it seemed he'd finally found a significant error. The floor joists were all a half-inch east of where they should be. He wrote a check for the two weeks' worth of work we'd done, turned his back to us, and began curling up a length of extension cord. We loaded our tools and left.

I hate to admit this, but I was relieved. Amy and I have lived without running water for almost a year now, and my paychecks were to get us a real shower and even a flush toilet. But building had taken my best, most energetic time and left me with little or nothing for writing at the end of each day. I'm a greedy man when it comes to writing time and energy, I'm afraid.

I suppose I'm a product of my family. My father and two of his brothers, all of whom worked the ranch in their youth, now write, daily. My grandfather even writes on trees. His "date trees" he calls them. They are, in fact, birches—an entire grove of birches, their parchment-like skins covered with wax pencil recordings of each day's news. Generally, his inscriptions note the weather—"6-11-90 Yeah! Sunshine!" and up high on the trunks, where he had reached by standing on the snow, "1-15-88 Blizzard. Finally cleared this a.m." Also in black wax pencil are family events—"Jon arrives on train tonight" and "Sheila and Ronny anniversary."

That grove of peeling birch bark journal entries is out there right now, wound like strands of DNA or etch-scribed marble columns in some fantastic temple dedicated to the holy art of contemplation, and to marking the days, and to solitude. To writing.

Still, losing my job was humbling. I'd worked hard, and we needed the money. Later the morning I was fired, as I drove Amy into town, to her work, I told her this, and she took my hand. "I'm glad you'll have all day for poems now," she said with kindness and a touch of sympathy in her voice.

We passed the heron that lives down on Westmond Creek—the same stretch of creek that had been swollen with meltwater many weeks before, and where during the New Year's rains, the current had nearly washed out the bridge. Now the water flowed healthy but slow around the heron's feet. I'd seen the bird every morning on my way down to work and had always envied his coming day, his unworried leisure. Or, perhaps it was his stillness I envied, his perfect solitude, the way he belonged to the landscape.

"Look at him," I said to Amy. "He's got all day for poems."

"Or she," Amy said playfully. Then, in a completely different tone, she said, "I'd be about eight months."

I'm often caught off guard by Amy's sudden comments about the baby. I think she has to say such things in the midst of other talk, has to deliver her grief into speech in an unmarked package, like a little bomb, so that she can speak it at all. Her eyes teared up just as suddenly. "I'd even be off bed rest. Everything would be okay if she'd made it this far."

"I know," I said, wishing I could match the empathy she'd showed me only a few moments before over something as insignificant as getting fired. "You miss her so much," I said.

She nodded.

"Me too."

Amy sighed, "So how are you going to spend your day?"

"I honestly don't know yet."

"That's nice."

"Yeah, it is," I readily agreed. "Still, I'm sorry about this, about losing the income."

"I'm not. It wasn't worth it."

"I just wish I could give you some stability."

"Well, you did build our house."

"I know," I said. "We did, together."

"And," she added with a pat on my knee, "it's only been a few weeks since your grant ran out. You'll find something good."

"I should be consoling you."

"You do," she said.

My cousin Heidi, beautiful and twenty, with long blond hair that rises off her shoulders when she shows me how to sit while in a gallop. She's spent much of her life on a horse, and in two days she would be leaving to move in with her boyfriend in an apartment in Laramie, Wyoming. My lesson would likely be her last chance to ride for months.

I rode okay, even through a warm, afternoon cloudburst. At least I stayed in my saddle despite the slick rain as Chico galloped and tossed his head, toying with me, asserting himself, a big Norwegian Fjord, against my obvious inexperience with the reins. "You have to let go a little. If you hold on too tight he knows you're worried to lose control," Heidi called over as she passed me bareback on Chico's sister, Chiquita.

"Let go a little," I repeated to myself.

A few yards ahead of me Heidi dug her heels into Chiquita and seemed to lift into the air as the horse lowered itself into a flat-out run. The wet valley floor rumbled with the noise of hoofbeats and freedom, and I loosened my grip on Chico's reins.

Through the Spokane Airport coffee shop window I watched the plane climb and bank over the open prairie horizon of eastern Washington and head south. Amy was on that plane, flying to Boise for a social-work conference. In front of the security gate next to me, a group of high schoolers, a chorus on their way to Europe, sang a song for the local TV cameras. They all had on matching shirts with *Cheney High School* and *Europe Tour* on the back. Parents hugged them and slipped them extra twenty-dollar bills. Camera flashes went off.

Pulling onto the highway toward Idaho, the little cab of our truck seemed enormously empty, and the radio only replayed the news, stories we'd heard together hours before on our way down. At that moment, what I wanted most out of the future was to be in it, and for Amy to be in it with me. What a fragile thing it is to be alive and together.

Two days before, we'd been reminded just how fragile while hiking in the high country of the Cabinet Mountains Wilderness. We'd come to a river crossing at Placer Creek, an upper tributary of the East Fork of the Bull River. In a month that creek would probably be only a stream, crossable with a few short hops from stone to stone, but right then it was a torrent, a raging, white rapids of snowmelt. There was still snow up in those mountains, snow in the woods under the canopy of massive old growth cedar and larch, snow on the face and rocky spine of St. Paul Peak, snow melting in millions of tons an hour in the June sun.

I walked over Placer Creek on a deadfall log, left my daypack on the far bank, and came back to lead Yukon across. Yukon did great crossing the log as long as there was bark for traction under his big paws. Over the most violent section of the river, though, the bark was off the log, and Yukon's muddy paws slipped, first a front one and a back one on either side. Then, when he had both front paws back on the log and was struggling to get the rest of himself back up, both his back legs went over one side.

Amy screamed from the shore and in one motion I straddled the log and grabbed the shaggy fur of his lower back, hoisting him up on the log.

"Oh my God!" Amy screamed over the roar of water. "Oh my God!" and she brought her hands to her mouth.

Wrapping my legs around the log as I'd been learning to do with a horse, I put my arms under Yukon's belly, lifted him to my chest, and slid backward, pushing against the log with my boot heels.

When I was safely across, Amy followed. We sat on the ground stroking him as he panted and looked from one of us to the other and back as if to say, "What, exactly, was that?"

We were across and had hours of daylight left. I figured we'd find a safer crossing on the way down so we hiked on. Trouble was, when we returned to the river on our descent hours later, we found no safer crossing. We had only two water bottles, a headlamp, and a camera, and it was getting dark. No one else knew where we were, and ours had been the only vehicle parked on the Forest Service road four miles below when we started out.

We agreed there was no getting Yukon back across that log. We hiked through thick underbrush and devil's club needles looking for a crossing, but all we found was one narrows, perhaps twenty feet across, where the water looked *maybe* three feet deep—though it was hard to tell through the milky, mineral-rich rush of water.

I headed across with my daypack, trying to test my footings as I went and, at the same time, push against the river current, which was threatening to knock me off balance and downstream into a churning cauldron of water, rocks, and logs. I made it to the other side, dropped my pack without celebration, headed back across, and picked up Yukon, who whined and kicked a bit. I expected the dog's 120 pounds to just about tip the balance in the river's favor. But after I kissed Amy and stepped back into the frigid water, I found that his weight actually helped keep my legs planted against the current.

When I got across and plopped him down, I noticed I'd left Yukon's leash on, and I realized suddenly how stupid I had been. Had we fallen in, the leash could well have gotten caught on a snag and held him in the water. However, the leash, an eight-foot length of climbing rope, did turn out to be the perfect thing to help Amy across. I unclipped it and stepped in the river again. Grabbing hold of a sapling, I waded out about halfway, tossed the other end of the leash to Amy, and pulled her along as she crossed the swiftest few feet. Safe on the riverbank, we danced and hugged and shouted and Yukon jumped up on us and licked our faces.

Three hours later we sat in the Hereford Bar on Highway 200, scarfing down pizza, our wet legs finally warming and our toes curling in our wet socks with each absurdly delicious bite. We even bought a big, $2/3$-pound Hereford Burger and took it out to Yukon in the pickup.

Alive. I've had a couple close calls in past years when I used to climb rock, moments spent falling at the end of a slack rope that seemed to take a lifetime to twang tight, and the feeling afterward, for days, was much the same as what I've been feeling since the crossing at Placer Creek. The world is suddenly forgiven all its disappointments and sorrows. The air tastes sharp, steely with adrenaline and love.

Back from the airport, with only Yukon's eyes to follow me around the cabin as he lay on the floor, I cleaned. "She's in Boise by now, boy," I said and swept the floor, changed the sheets on our bed, collected our breakfast bowls, and wiped down the little table. Everything in the cabin—floor, table, bowls, even Yukon—all of it seemed new, part of a future Amy and I would be living in together.

Three days after watching her leave, I watched Amy's plane from Boise land and taxi up the runway. I had news for her.

Seeing that plane pull up to the terminal, jet turbines spinning down and quieting, and the long arm of the boarding corridor extending toward the door, I can honestly say I felt right. Right, not necessarily healed. Not recovered. Simply right.

Amy and I kissed like shameless high schoolers with the other passengers passing around us. Then I told her about a job I'd landed. It was writing for the *River Journal* newspaper, a bimonthly that covers a territory from our own Westmond all the way to Thompson Falls, Montana, ninety miles east of us. We'd met the paper's editor, Dennis, this winter and he and I had taken a couple snowshoes and hikes together. "Dennis decided to open a Sandpoint editorial office," I said. "I saw him at Safeway and he asked for a writing sample; then yesterday he left a message on Steve and Marguerite's answering machine."

"That's great," Amy said. "Better than building a house for some guy who follows you around with a tape measure all day."

I told her that the job didn't pay great, and there were no benefits, but it was close to full-time.

"I can't wait to read your first piece," she said and we held hands as we walked to the baggage carousel.

Later, in the parking garage, I set her suitcase down and chased her as our laughs and footfalls echoed off the concrete pillars and walls. Spinning around between two parked cars, she let me catch her, and we kissed again.

Earlier this spring Amy spent several weeks looking for a group for parents who'd lost babies, but there was no such group in little Sandpoint. So instead, we've been going to a group for parents whose children have died. At first, we were worried that it would be a bad fit, that we wouldn't be able to relate to the other people there, the parents. But just the opposite happened, especially for Amy, who, every week, told me how comforting the group was for her, how the other parents had helped her feel Hannah *was* a real baby. And while what we'd lost was different from what they'd lost, they welcomed us as one of their own.

This week we were supposed to bring letters we composed to our children. The group meeting place at the Bonner County Hospice Building was an old living room, complete with plants on the fireplace mantel, white upright piano, and a window that overlooked a yard of grass and trees. We'd become comfortable there over the weeks, as we'd become comfortable with one another, chatting before group started as we sat there in a circle on sofas, overstuffed recliners, and kitchen chairs.

It was June 25th, wedding anniversary number three for Amy and me and a birthday for one of the group members, so we ate cake off of little paper plates as we asked one another how the week went, how our gardens, building projects, vacations, and jobs were going. Everyone had read my first articles in the latest issue of the *River Journal*, and they all had kind things to say about my writing. Someone asked Amy how things were at the shelter and she told them it was pretty full as usual. They shook their heads and someone said she's sure doing important work there, something that's been needed in northern Idaho for years. We could have easily been mistaken for a group of neighbors gathered at one of our houses, just some ordinary neighborhood parents getting together and eating cake and making small talk before the conversation takes its inevitable turn toward our children.

Then it was time to start. We dropped our paper plates and plastic forks into the garbage can beneath the kitchen sink and reassembled quietly in our circle. We took turns reading our letters. The words rose through each reader's throat like song, and though tears flowed all around, each voice was unwavering, the low, loving tone of parent to child, steady even in saying good-bye.

When it was Amy's turn she started "Dear Bean," using the nickname—as she paused and looked up over the top of her letter to explain—because that was the name by which she knew our daughter longest. "This is the most difficult letter I've ever written."

She sighed a heavy sigh filled with a resignation I'd never heard in her before and straightened herself in her chair. Her eyes locked onto the words on the page, and she began again:

> I've envisioned my life with you and I don't know how to quit thinking of my life with you so suddenly. I've thought of the walks we'd take, the talks we'd have, the time together we'd have. I've thought of taking you home from the hospital, holding your hand when you take your first steps, feeding you with a spoon for the first time, the funny faces you'd make when you would eat something you didn't like. I've thought of hiking with you in a baby carrier. I've thought of watching you sleep and holding you when you wake.
>
> I've thought of your first day of kindergarten and class plays. I've tried to think of your personality and the voice you'd have. I've thought of your first Christmas and watching you breathe as you sleep.
>
> I thought that I'd be able to hold you for hours. I thought that I would be able to crawl with you, play with you, dance with you, sing with you. We won't be able to do those things.
>
> I won't ever hold you, rock you, play with you, dance with you.
>
> I feel gypped, and I want you back so we can play out my fantasies and dreams.
>
> Hannah, you are in a peaceful place now—a place where

no harm will ever come to you. A place that I don't know and don't understand.

Everything in this world that I experience or see reminds me of you. Everything I experience reminds me that you won't experience anything. And things I see remind me that you will never see.

I'm confused and scared and so sorry you will never get a chance in life.

You only knew my womb as your life and it's probably better that way, better you weren't born only to die in a couple hours, but I wish it were different.

I want to hold you and watch you take breaths. I want to look into your eyes and see you look back at me. I want to touch your hand and feel you touch back. I want to hear you make baby sounds and listen to you cry. I want to feel your baby smooth skin and smell your baby smells.

I want to tell you how special you are and have you hear it. I love you, Hannah, Bean.

I'm not sure how to keep living my life without you. You were my future. You kept me going when things became difficult, when I got down. I don't know how to plan my life without planning for your arrival.

I left the hospital after I gave birth to you, without you.

You were born but you didn't cry. You couldn't see, you didn't breathe, and you couldn't move.

You were too small, not viable the doctors and nurses said. No immune system.

My milk came for you, but because you weren't here to take it, it went away, dried up, and didn't return.

I love you, Bean.

I love you, Hannah.

Hannah Marjorie Howko-Johnson. Born and died on March 8 at 2:55 a.m.

Premature.
10 inches. 12 ounces.
I miss you.

I sat in the devastation of Amy's loss for a long time, absorbing her words as she sat with the letter folded in her lap. All of us stared at the floor in the center of our circle.

The only thing I wanted was to keep sitting in that room, in the love and shared grief of the people there, people who say Hannah's name often. No one in the group wanted to move. It was as if we were waiting for our children, who were somewhere outside, somewhere just beyond our view out the big picture window, playing together in the summer twilight.

Carlson's Field sold. For the record, Billy was asking $160,000 and got $120,000, twice what he paid for the land (with all its timber uncut) two years ago.

But regardless of the economics, the field sold. The new owner is an Alaskan bush pilot, the realtor told me, who plans to build one dwelling, his own retirement home, and hide out up there.

I've decided the world will not change much if some retired Alaskan pilot builds up in that field. The world will not be less in the way it is less without our child.

We've got our little cabin on land I've come to think of as an extension of my own body, land my family has lived on and lived off for more than forty years. That will be more than enough for Amy and me to build a life on. I will not create sorrows in a life where sorrows find me on their own.

And the good news was the bush pilot doesn't plan to build for at least three years. For three years the field will be ours to hike and picnic on and sneak up to late at night for romantic moon rises. I'll be able to wander up there, into that grass now as high as my shoulders, and stand on the spot where I began to mourn Hannah.

In the course of three years Amy and I could have another baby, and that baby could sleep beside us there, in the sun, on a blanket spread over a bed of hay. Three years. The field will not be ours forever. But no place on earth ever is.

Amy's been bringing home baby clothes again. She'll stop off at the secondhand store and pick up a tiny jumper with Winnie the Pooh on the chest or an infant-size dress covered with sunflowers. She keeps these things at the bottom of our steamer trunk, under our quilts and blanket. Before she puts them away, she shows them to me, unsnapping and resnapping the front, or holding up the outfit by the shoulders.

Hannah would have been born any day now, if she'd made it to full term.

Sometimes we both think maybe we ought to just go for it—forget the grieving process and the insurance and health worries—and just start trying for another child. But we want our next child to have his or her own start, to have the benefits of Amy on complete bed rest and of specialized prenatal care that, had we known about Amy's cervix earlier, could have possibly saved Hannah. And, perhaps just as important, we want our next child to have parents who are healed and optimistic, who have recovered some measure of the innocent, welcoming hearts of first parents—though we can never go all the way back and wouldn't if we could. Hannah will always be our firstborn.

For the first time in more than a month, I got something done on the cabin. I took off early from work at the newspaper office and drove the half-hour back up to the ranch, working out in my head how the pine tongue-and-groove boards should be cut to fit the odd corners and angles of one of the kitchen walls. Having that hammer in my hand and seeing the tangible effects of my will as each bright blond, swirl-grained, pine board took its permanent place, I felt inside my life again.

That wall would be the wall of our kitchen and our children's kitchen. The laughter of my family would fall on its wood. We would dance a baby around the room and cast our lamp-lit shadows on that wall. It seemed like much longer than four months since I'd had such thoughts.

I have crossed the Cabinet Mountains, a sixteen-mile walk from just outside the town of Libby, Montana, to the Bull River Valley. Five thousand feet up and over and five thousand feet down in a day.

My hiking partner was Dennis, my editor at the newspaper, who'd first mentioned a trip into the Cabinets when we met this past winter. To Dennis the high country is a guiding principle. Since he moved to Montana from Virginia fresh out of high school twenty years ago, he has organized his entire life around spending as many afternoons as possible up in the subalpine fir and snowfields. And, when he is in the valley below, he spends a good chunk of his time writing about higher elevations.

Dennis has no wife, no children, does not own even one square foot of property, and drives a battered old Chevy Suburban. He can tell you the Latin and common names of every wildflower and moss in the Cabinet Mountains Wilderness. He can make the life cycle of the rare white bark pine sound like a goddess-myth of fire and ice, perseverance, catastrophe, and triumph. As the trail climbed through a stand of those high-altitude trees, I thought how, up ahead of me, Dennis looked a little like a white bark pine himself—tall and lean, a native species. And I wondered if I would ever belong so completely to the wilderness.

It was a little over one year ago that Amy and I were on the AlCan Highway getting further and further into Alaska by the mile. The pickup was loaded down with books and dishes and winter clothes, and Amy and I were filled with unchecked enthusiasm. We'd spent the previous year getting ready. We were four months ahead on our truck payments, had cleared all the credit cards and even socked away a couple thousand dollars to last us until we found jobs. And in the backs of our minds was the notion of a baby.

We drove all day every day, singing and planning into the late evening sun, then camped in the woods each night under a sky that never darkened past dusk. The entire summer we lived out of the back of the pickup, cooking on the tailgate and sitting on stumps.

Our windshield still has its chips from the AlCan gravel, and the cabin we returned to finish is closing in on being done. Losing Hannah has changed us, has shown us limitation and taught us about unanswered longing. But we still have our lives to live. We still have each other and our dream of a life in the wilderness and even of a baby. That much has survived.

A few hundred feet above tree line the slopes were peppered with wildflowers. Dennis and I paused to suck greedily on our water bottles and look down on a tiny cobalt, glacial lake in a bowl of mountains, one of which we were ascending. He picked a delicate yellow wildflower from the grass and popped it in his mouth with a grin.

"Glacier lily!" he said, chewing.

With his wire-rimmed glasses and sandy blond hair, he

looked a little like a tall version of John Denver, and I recalled how he'd once told me it was partly Denver's music that put the idea of moving to the Rockies in his head when he was still a boy in Virginia.

"They're very nutritious," he said, picking another glacier lily. "And good."

I picked one and ate it. Dennis was right. The petals were soft and thin, but the sweet, full taste of nectar filled my mouth.

We pressed on, one foot methodically up and planted on the trail above the other, until the rut of trail in the grass disappeared into jumbled talus rock rattling loosely under our boots. We skirted snowdrifts still fifteen feet tall, the snow dirty from windblown dust and pockmarked from months of daytime sun and night freezes.

At the summit of Dome Mountain, we let our daypacks slide off our shoulders and sat down. Dennis pointed out each major landform in sight, every creek drainage and ridge between the Kootenai River to the north, and A-Peak, Snowshoe, and Ibex Mountains to the south. He swept his long arm over the landscape like a wind and pointed. "That's Cedar Creek, and over the next rise is the North Fork of the Bull."

When Dennis wandered a ways away with his binoculars and map to survey future hike routes, I leaned back on the rocks, propped my head against my pack, and closed my eyes. When I opened them again, I took in the bottoms of clouds, a landscape of clouds to the horizon, hung in a blue sky and just a few thousand feet over peaks and ridges without end.

The next day would be Hannah's due date. The eighteenth of July. Odds are she would not have been born on her due date (few people are, Dr. Bowden had told us as we grinned at her seven months ago, our eyes on that paper-wheel calendar in her hand), but July 18th is what Amy and I are left with.

So what now? Caution? Predictable moves only? A stack of résumés to put in the mail for well-paying, fully benefited university jobs? How do we take this consuming desire for a child and simply trust our lives to unfold as they will? How do we grow up without growing prematurely old?

The answer, of course, is that we have no choice but to trust our lives again, to follow what has always been an unknown route.

Dennis and I descended off Dome Mountain, down Taylor Ridge, over steep snowfields and through stands of alpine larch—miniature, gnarled versions of their lowland cousins, the trees that make up our cabin logs. The alpine larch grow in small clusters and were only just starting to open their waxy, bright green needle buds for a two- or three-month growing season. Looking back at the peak from a field of skin-soft pine grass, I couldn't believe the distance we'd covered in just a few minutes. The valley floor was still thousands of feet below us, but already the summit above looked enormous, imposing but far off, seen all at once after turning around.

I remembered the glacier lily on the other side, how the powder yellow flower had turned to sweet pulp between my tongue and the roof of my mouth, how the stem tasted like grass dipped in honey.

We walked through the ruins of a burned forest, past a few scorched and sun-bleached trunks still standing in the new fields around us. There another flower bloomed, one I had noticed on our way up and that Dennis now informed me was called death camas. It grew up in paler yellow, almost white blossoms among the fireweed, purple beardtongue, larkspur, bear grass, and more glacier lilies on this side of the mountain.

"Don't eat those unless you absolutely want to die," Dennis said admiringly as he crouched close to a tuft of the delicate flowers.

These live here too, I thought, crouching beside him and taking the stem of one in my fingers, but not picking it. They grow from the same soil, in the same sunny, thin, cool air as the glacier lilies in my guts and already starting to become human flesh.

Today is the nineteenth of July, the day after Hannah's due date. It's a brilliant morning, the sun tilting over the cool forest on the slope of Butler Mountain and across the valley below. Amy is out walking the ranch with Yukon. She is photographing the fields of full-bloom daisies and the sun filtering through grand fir needles, the tufts of moss growing on forty-year-old fence posts—a whole world that seems to wait for a child.

Last night we took down the funeral candle, Hannah's ashes, and the glass-and-tile mosaic our families made at the memorial service. We lit the candle and placed it in the big picture window beside the log urn and the mosaic. It was a full moon, the biggest moon I've ever seen, searching the valley with blue-white light. The tips of trees and the profile of Butler Mountain stood out in dark silhouette against the bright night sky. The candle reflected its steady point of flame off the glass.

Where have we come? I have never in life been so uncertain of what I ought to be doing, of what I should center my life around. I remember winter, when this cabin was a tiny boat in a storm. Now we'll have to learn what foreign beach we've washed up on.

When I think of the future, I think of children, fatherhood. I think of teaching jobs, pulling up to this cabin door after a two-day drive from some far-off university town, unpacking a week's worth of groceries and one grocery sack full of bright toys. I think of Amy finally carrying a baby through that door. I will remember this time, remember waiting here for Bean, whispering that nickname into Amy's belly. Here I will feel closest to the lost soul of my firstborn. When I am an old man, if I make it to that territory, I will sit at this kitchen table and leaf through these pages, the pages of Hannah's story.

As Amy and I sat on the couch holding each other and stared into the candle, we said out loud what we would have done with our daughter, how we'd have loved her into this life.

"I would have read her *Goodnight Moon*."

"She would have had more books than you."

"I would have walked the woods with her on my back."

"I would have danced with her."

"I would have washed her back in the chilly water of Lake Superior."

"I would have told her I love her fifty times a day."

"I would have held her."

"I would have nursed her."

"I would have watched her sleep."

Our voices drifted over the dark, impenetrable log walls.

At night, when I am lying awake late in bed—as I did last night on what would have been my daughter's birthday, her funeral candle blown out, her ashes and mosaic back up on the shelf—I often hear trains winding down the twin rails two miles away.

Around midnight the passenger train, with its sleeping travelers and dimly green-lit interior, slips through our valley. When I heard the distant rumble and calling horn of last night's train I felt certain it was that train, the train with people on board, its strobe light flashing on low bows and trackside weeds, answering the steady moon like a heartbeat speaking to an eardrum. As I sometimes do, I dreamed Hannah was on that train, passing through this country, passing so close to her parents, her life out just beyond the first rows of trees passing into dark.

Postpartum

But dreamin' just comes natural,
like the first breath from a baby.
— John Prine

Two years later . . .

I crossed the Great Divide driving a U-Haul pulling our old, blue pickup on a flatbed trailer. Amy and Yukon followed in a red, only-slightly-less-old Toyota 4Runner we'd recently purchased used in the hopes that we'd need a vehicle with a back seat before long. Yukon had his head out the passenger window. I caught glimpses of him in my oversized side mirrors. His ears flapped in the wind and nose lifted into the late September mountain air, the first he'd smelled in almost two years.

It was evening. The sun slipped down the sides of the steep canyon walls and lit the tops of tamarack and Douglas fir and quaking aspen. I drove with bare feet and my elbow out the window. We were going west. Home to Idaho.

We'd left the December after losing Hannah. That fall we'd learned that Amy was pregnant again. But at her twelve-week checkup, Margaret Bowden couldn't find the baby's heartbeat.

"It doesn't necessarily mean anything," she said, finally setting the fetal microphone down on the counter. "It's most likely just a little too soon for this one. Still, I'm going to see if I can get you in for an ultrasound, just so we can be sure."

"But it might not be just that it's too early?" Amy asked and sat up.

"It might not be, but it might. Probably we're wrong about how far along you are. We'll know as soon as I can get you in."

She got us in right away, to the same dark ultrasound room we'd been in when we discovered that Amy's cervix was opening beneath Hannah—"funneling" we've since learned such a change is called, after the cone shape the weak cervix takes on as the opening at the uterus grows wider and deeper and the remaining closed cervix gets shorter and shorter. It's the shape of a tornado, a vortex into which a life can fall like a star into a black hole.

But for this pregnancy that complication was still weeks away, after seventeen or eighteen weeks' gestation, when the baby and bag of waters gets large and heavy enough to stretch and put pressure on the cervix. Now that we knew about Amy's predisposition for the problem, we had a plan. Margaret was going to perform a cerclage, putting a stitch in the cervix to keep it from funneling too deeply, and Amy was going to spend all the following months of her pregnancy reclining.

Only, the faces of the ultrasound technician and the radiologist beside her were telling us otherwise. The technician had just started the procedure, holding the sensor to Amy's belly as Amy and I held hands and all four of us stared at the monitor, when Amy asked the radiologist, "You don't see a heartbeat, do you?"

"No. I'm sorry. I'm so sorry, I don't."

The grief was crushingly familiar. Tears ran down Amy's face as she lay on an examining table. We were told that the baby had died in the womb as much as a week before and its body had already broken down to the point that the ultrasound showed no features, no arms or legs or head. That, or the fetus hadn't ever formed properly. Either way, Amy would most likely miscarry very soon.

And she did. On a drizzly day in November, our second baby, the one we'd been calling Tiny Baby, came to us in the cabin loft as unrecognizable blood clots.

I built a fire outside as Amy had asked. "I want to keep this baby's ashes with Hannah's," she'd told me when she first felt the cramps start.

Hannah's ashes. Our summer visit to Marquette was long over, and we still hadn't spread them in Lake Superior.

When the thin sticks of cedar kindling flared up I put in pieces of seasoned birch. Strips of the white bark peeled back like burning pages as they turned to flame. When the fire had burned down and hot to a pile of orange ash and blocks of glowing birch, I placed a crumpled handful of tissues wrapped around what remained of Tiny Baby on the spade of a shovel, which I then held in the center of the bed of coals.

Though my hair and skin were wet with cold drizzle and I could now hear the fizz of drops of rain hitting the embers, the air close in to the fire was scalding on my hands and face as I leaned over it, holding the shovel.

In seconds the tissue on the spade blossomed into flame. In a few seconds more there was only ash, which I poured into a coffee can and covered to cool and keep dry.

We left Idaho a month later. Our dream of raising a child in our cabin in the midst of the mountain wilderness had, we told ourselves, finally been beaten completely out of us. We'd return for short trips, maybe even bring a child to visit some day (Margaret had said the miscarriage was a terrible coincidence, unrelated to the loss of Hannah and to Amy's incompetent cervix). But as we swept the floor and threw white sheets over the furniture, we thought we'd never live in the cabin again.

We moved back to Michigan, where I spent the winter searching for academic jobs across the country. We were willing to go almost anywhere I could get good medical insurance and earn enough for Amy to stay home for bed rest through a pregnancy. What I found was a job teaching at a small Presbyterian college in the Appalachian coal country of southwestern Pennsylvania.

We rented a house two blocks from the campus of colonial, red-brick and whitewashed buildings, ancient oak trees, and close-trimmed lawns. Though the college was conservative and my dean (a tall, gaunt, white-haired, old Christian academic with a face that made me think of a bird of prey staring down at students and faculty) told me I ought to "look more dignified and less shaggy," I loved teaching. One of my courses was Nature in Literature, which I often met outside on the grass in the shade of those oaks. I might have been wearing a tie and worrying that the dean would stroll by, stop in to listen, and disapprove of my informal, discussion-based teaching style, but still, I was getting *paid* to sit cross-legged outside, talking about Wordsworth and Emerson, Thoreau and John Muir with nineteen- and twenty-year-olds.

And in many ways besides just my teaching, Pennsylvania offered us the new start we'd needed. Amy found a job doing social work at a hospital and we began paying off the debt we'd incurred building the cabin. We found a community of friends among some of the other new faculty members and their families.

In under a year I'd gone from the low-wage, uncertain work of a carpenter and small-town newspaper writer to the middle-class life of a professor with a good salary, full family health coverage, an oversized sport utility vehicle, a comfortable house in town, friends, and what I considered a silly amount of social standing. (After they'd learned what I did from the college logo on my check stubs, the little old lady tellers at the bank would say "Good morning, Professor" when I walked though the door.)

We were getting exactly what we'd wanted out of leaving Idaho, including, when we were ready, another shot at having a baby. But by midwinter I was the most depressed I'd been in my life. I hadn't written a poem since taking the job. I spent all my passion and energy on my classes only to come home and stare out the window of my study at the thin layer of soggy snow on the street. I thought about Butler Mountain. That powdery Rocky Mountain snow that moved across the valley and fell for days was probably falling at that very moment, on the limbs of fir and on the cabin roof and in the alfalfa field and in Carlson's Field. I grew my hair and beard long and often wore hiking boots and jeans in defiance of the dean. I swore occasionally in class to my students' delight. But by Hannah's second birthday on March 8th, I was in a free fall.

One day when I *had* worn a blazer and tie and loafers I saw the dean walking across the courtyard, and as we passed he pivoted his head, the eagle spotting prey, and said, "Ah, it looks like Dr. Johnson, but he's got a tie on."

I nodded and smiled, went home, kicked half the spindles out of the stair banister, and punched holes in the louvered doors of the bedroom closet.

And Amy wasn't much happier. Though her job paid twice what she'd been making directing the shelter in Sandpoint, she now had to answer to hospital administrators, insurance companies, and doctors. She missed living in the forest almost as much as I did, missed the quiet nights and the constant company of the mountains. She would call Deb in Idaho late at night to hear about the huckleberry picking in the mountains or the moose that had wandered into the yard. Deb had taken over Amy's position as director of the domestic violence shelter and she'd ask Amy for advice about handling a drunk client or a staff problem. There would be a pause and Amy'd say, "I wish I could," and I'd know Deb had offered to give Amy her old job back as she did every time they talked, if only we'd return.

Even Yukon was miserable. While he loved the attention my students would lavish on him when I walked him on campus, he spent most of his time curled on a window seat watching cars pass.

"One more year," Amy and I told each other. "We'll hold on for one more year and leave Pennsylvania with a baby," we'd say lying in bed as the slivers of light from headlights swept across the ceiling. Where we'd go next we didn't know, but it had to be someplace else I could work since Amy wanted to stay home the first year of the baby's life. Maybe if we were very lucky, some university in the northwest or in northern Minnesota or Wisconsin. "Something within a day's drive of the cabin or our parents would be nice," Amy said.

Though the hunt for a new job was another year away, I started checking the advertisements anyway. I'd close my office door after letting out my last class for the day and get on the Internet to keep up on what sorts of positions were available, and how many, and above all where.

What I saw only depressed me further, jobs in places like New Jersey and Indiana, places without mountains or wilderness or elk or twenty-foot snowfalls. And many of the ads requested applications only from poets with two or more books. I'd only recently learned that my first book was accepted for publication.

Then, toward the end of the winter I read a job ad that made my heart race as the words registered in my head. It was for an emerging poet with a minimum of one book to teach for a year in the Master of Fine Arts Program at Eastern Washington University in downtown Spokane. It was a program with a reputation I knew well. I'd read work by every one of the faculty writers, some of whom I'd long considered among the best writers of not only that region but the entire country.

And downtown Spokane was sixty miles from our cabin. *Sixty miles!*

I applied for the job without allowing myself to even briefly entertain the fantasy that I might get it. But in early summer the phone rang and when I picked it up the voice on the other end of the line was John Keeble, the head of the program. I knew whole paragraphs of his fiction by heart.

He asked if I was still interested in the job and when I said something absurd like, "My God, yes," he said he'd call soon to set up a phone interview.

By the end of the summer Amy and I were packing a U-Haul. We'd investigated the maternity benefits at Eastern Washington University and found them excellent, and we'd called people at the hospitals in Spokane for information about their high-risk pregnancy services, which sounded good. Amy gave notice at her job at the hospital, and when I told the dean I'd be moving on, he said I'd sure be missed, though his face was filled with relief when he shook my hand. I suspect I might have been grinning.

And 2,300 miles later, as I wound the U-Haul down US 2 from Marias Pass, Montana, the vast expanse of Glacier Park on the other side of the battered guardrail on my right and the Great Bear Wilderness just past the gravel shoulder to my left, I was the happiest I'd been since we'd learned Amy was pregnant with Hannah.

The weight of the pickup on the trailer gave slight shoves and then tugs now and then so I drove slow—thirty-five, forty miles an hour through those tight curves, in and out of the canyon shade. There was no rush. We'd make the cabin by midnight.

Within a month, Amy would be pregnant again.

That fall I did more driving, down an hour of mountain roads and another twenty minutes of freeway into Spokane to teach.

My office was half the size of our entire cabin, with a wall of windows that looked out over downtown and the mountains at the Idaho border from which I'd just come. My door had a plaque with my name on it.

I'd call Amy to tell her I'd made the commute in okay and ask her how she was feeling—which was usually nauseous and tired, but so happy and hopeful about this new pregnancy. I'd teach my classes, go out to a tavern for one beer with the students, then start the long drive home, my head buzzing not from the drink but from the electricity among those writers, adults from all over the country who'd come to the program to study, whose passion for poetry had so governed their lives that they'd moved hundreds and often thousands of miles to join that community of writers.

Amy and I threw a big party at the cabin and invited those students along with my colleagues on the faculty, our Idaho friends, and my family. Dozens and dozens of cars were parked tucked in among the trees and in the meadows along the road up to the cabin, and the cabin was packed to overflowing. People stood out on the new deck I'd built and hiked with my uncle Steve over to the Back Slope. I grilled hamburgers and steaks from cows raised on our ranch and my students teased me about being a vegetarian who helped raise and then served beef. Kids ran up and down the loft stairs and my grandparents sat in rocking chairs, telling John and Claire Keeble about buying the place and moving to Idaho with a young family.

John and Claire where the same age as our parents and had become fast friends with Amy and me. When they were young and John was newly hired at the university, they'd built their own log house on three hundred acres outside Spokane and raised three children there. We were inspired by them—Claire, who was an accomplished violist in the Spokane Symphony but who, off stage, mostly wore hiking boots, an untucked flannel shirt, and her wavy gray hair down, and John, with his straw hat and cowboy boots, a mustache hiding the top half of his grin when my grandfather told him how good it was to have another generation putting down roots on the homeplace.

When the sky got dark and the air cold, I built a fire in a pit in the alfalfa field and people sat around it on bales of hay and passed a bottle of wine, swigging from the jug. Hours later I wandered away from the fire to take a leak over at the edge of the woods and when I turned around to walk back I was amazed. This was my life. Those were my new and old friends under the rising swirl of sparks, Amy was pregnant somewhere in the midst of those laughing voices, and the two of us were back here again, taking another shot at our dream.

Over Christmas break we moved down to Spokane. Our apartment was in a handsome, eighty-year-old brick building and had hardwood floors and got lots of afternoon sun in which Amy could grow houseplants and herbs. We only had to sign a lease through June, by which time, if all went well, the baby would be born and we'd be moving back into the cabin. Meanwhile, we'd be a half-mile from the building in which I taught and had my office, and it was just three blocks beyond that to the hospital we'd chosen for Amy's care. Despite Deb's offer to give Amy her old position back (or *any* kind of position she wanted at the shelter, for that matter, Deb was so thrilled that we were back), Amy hadn't taken a job when we returned to Idaho, so she had no obligations to disentangle herself from now. We were determined to stack the odds in this baby's favor. We'd use every lesson losing Hannah had taught us— no more bed rest in the cabin, no more dependence on Amy's income or insurance, no more unnecessary chances.

Amy spent hours on the phone researching to find the best perinatologist, as specialists in high-risk pregnancy are called. We wanted someone with an encyclopedic knowledge of up-to-the-moment practices in the specialty as well as a solid track record of getting difficult pregnancies to term. Amy found that and more in Cherie Johnson, a young woman who'd held multiple fellowships in the field and who now handled many of the toughest preterm labor and fetal distress cases flown in to Spokane by helicopter from as far away as eastern Montana. She was kind, too. She hugged each of us at least once every time we visited her office, which was just down the hall from the hospital's maternity unit, and she referred to Amy's cervix as "weak" rather than incompetent, a term she and Amy agreed must have been coined by a man. She called our baby "Pumpkin."

Dr. Johnson was from Philadelphia and wore Victorian dresses with high collars and rows of brass buttons. She kept her black hair in a straight bob cut precisely at her shoulders and though she always called herself Cherie, we couldn't help but call her Dr. Johnson. She was like an elegant, old-world magician whom we'd found to guide us through the dark forest of this pregnancy.

She held our hands from time to time when we must have looked uncertain or afraid, as I'm sure we did on December 31, the last day of the year and Amy's sixteenth week of pregnancy, up in the outpatient pre-op room, where she explained again the procedure she was about to do.

"I'll put two stitches in around the cervix," she said. "The studies are showing that two stitches around the cervix hold better than a single stitch. One down low and one a little bigger around and a little higher up. This is absolutely the best thing we can do to help keep this baby inside, guys. And Pumpkin won't even know any of this is going on."

We came home from the surgery to our apartment and, with the new year, began our siege. Dr. Johnson had said it was extremely unlikely Amy would make it to a full-term pregnancy of forty weeks but had encouraged us not to think that far head. Twenty-six weeks was the goal for now. Viability. She'd said we should be prepared for the possibility that Amy would end up in the hospital at some point, and that in the meantime she was to take Procardia orally every six hours to suppress contractions and limit activity to reclining most of the time.

We followed the orders knowing our child's life might well depend on how much Amy could keep off her feet. She wrote long lists of groceries for me to buy and plowed through book after thick book from the stack she'd been stockpiling for months. She wrote letters every day and organized pictures of the cabin's construction and our time in Pennsylvania in photo albums. Every evening I'd fix an involved dinner—steamed vegetables over wild rice, baked salmon with new potatoes and broccoli, red clam spaghetti. Nights I had to teach I'd put a portion for Amy on a plate and stick it in the microwave.

"Just push two minutes when you get hungry," I said once.

"I've used a microwave before."

"I know. I know. But don't get up for an extra trip if you can help it. Hit the timer when you have to get up anyway for the bathroom. And I'll get you a pitcher of water so you don't need to get up for that." How I hovered. I wasn't going to be helpless this time. I was going to do everything right.

"I want this baby to make it as much as you do," she'd say. "I'm not going to do anything to jeopardize it."

"I know you won't. You're doing amazing. You are my hero," I'd tell her and just before I'd leave for class I'd bend down to kiss her where she lay on the sofa, her back and side cushioned by pillows. Then I'd kiss her belly—which was only just starting to bulge—and say in a loud voice, as if speaking to someone in the next room, "Hellooooo Baby! We love you!"

"This baby will certainly know your voice," Amy'd say and I'd tell her that was the idea.

There was something in our tone when we'd talk of the baby coming, though, a hesitancy that would have been imperceptible to anyone besides us. We didn't give it a nickname right away as we had Bean and Tiny Baby, and we spoke less of what we'd do when this baby did come. Instead, we talked about every pregnancy symptom Amy was having, little cramps and tugs to which she was by now becoming much more attuned.

We kept our enthusiasm in check as time after time the weekly ultrasounds that Dr. Johnson ordered looked good. Amy's cervix stayed normal in appearance, a solid mass of light fuzz on the screen. We saw everything on the baby that was supposed to be there—except the gender, which we'd asked be kept a secret. The heart fluttered away. There were two legs tucked up against the belly, two arms with two little fists, a head.

At the end of the exams the technician would push a button and print us a picture of the baby. Dr. Johnson would stand and give each of us a hug and say, "Looks good, guys! One more week down. Real good news."

We'd thank her and smile, but on the drive home we were often quiet, as if afraid to voice the hope that was growing in us.

But as the baby grew so did our hope. Through January and into February the weeks added up—seventeen, eighteen, nineteen, twenty—far into the second trimester, until at twenty-one weeks, the same gestational point at which we'd lost Hannah, we saw the first sign of trouble.

The moment the image came on the screen Dr. Johnson said, "Well, darn it, guys, we're getting some funneling now."

There it was, that sliver of darkness inside the bright field of cervix. The black thread of a tornado spun from beneath a cloud silhouetted against a horizon of clear sky.

"Oh," Amy said and held a hand up to her mouth.

"This is what a weak cervix does," Dr. Johnson said, reaching over to touch Amy's shoulder but keeping her eyes on the monitor. "It's okay. See that upper stitch?" She touched the screen along a faint band of white. She looked at Amy now, moved her face in close to Amy's. "That stitch is holding fine. The funneling's not even close to that stitch yet, and there's a second stitch below that. You see it?"

Amy nodded through her tears.

"That's why they're in there. Now the stitches do their job. We've got a lot of options still and there's still some good closed cervix above the stitch. We're not at devastating. I want you to double your Procardia dose to 20 milligrams. Just to keep any contractions from starting. There are stretch receptors around the cervix where it joins the bottom of the uterus that can trigger labor contractions, so we'll keep ahead of that."

She finished the ultrasound and the baby looked fine, growing away, oblivious to the danger below. Amy sat up and I joined her on the exam table, wrapping my arm around her shoulder as Dr. Johnson told us she wanted to do ultrasounds twice a week for a while. Also, we should be vigilant about keeping Amy's activity limited. If she felt cramps or lower back pain or outright contractions, she should lie on her left side and drink lots and lots of water. That can calm the uterus muscles down. And she should recline even for meals. "Gravity's the enemy now, but this is nothing we aren't prepared for. We've got two stitches," she said, holding up two fingers as if in a sign of peace or victory.

Three days later, at the next ultrasound, the sliver of dark funneling was gone. The cervix looked normal again. Dr. Johnson said that wasn't surprising; the cervix was a dynamic structure. We'd keep a close eye on it, but for now the news was good.

We went home elated, but March 8th, Hannah's third birthday, loomed ahead of us. This baby would be twenty-four weeks by then, three weeks ahead of Hannah, but that was still hauntingly close in development and still probably not quite far enough along to survive outside. We did everything we could to distract ourselves from these realities and from the monotony of Amy's bed rest. We borrowed a television and learned the characters on shows every night of the week. We ordered takeout food from every Italian, Thai, and Chinese restaurant in downtown Spokane. On February 29th, we had a Leap Day/Amy's-been-on-bed-rest-two-months party at our apartment.

That afternoon, before our friends arrived, Amy reclined in her deck chair in the kitchen and talked me through each step as I chopped, poured, sprinkled, and stirred the ingredients of her favorite chili recipe into a kettle on the stove. She could only have a little as all the reclining made her prone to heartburn, but she said she was determined to eat some.

"I've been reading that the baby can taste in my amniotic fluid whatever I eat," she said and blew on a spoonful of chili to cool it.

"You're kidding."

"Nope. It said so in one of my pregnancy books." She ate the spoonful and smiled. "Delicious." She looked down at her tummy. "Just wait, little June Bug."

"June Bug?"

"It's due in June, so June Bug. I know I won't make it that far, but . . ." she shrugged.

"I like it anyway," I said.

"There's a song."

"A song?" I took down our plates and bowls from the cupboard and grabbed a fistful of spoons from the silverware drawer.

"The Baby June Bug Song," Amy said, feigning indifference as she blew on another spoonful of chili. She hadn't played like this, with this tone of someone with a great secret inside, since she was pregnant with Hannah. I went into the dining room and sat out the plates, bowls, and spoons. "I sing it sometimes when you're at school," she said from the kitchen.

I came back and crouched down beside her chair. "Can I hear it?"

Amy giggled and gave me a little push, throwing me off balance so I had to grab the floor. "Maybe later," she said.

Our friends, mostly writing students and faculty, showed up that night with dishes of their own to pass, and the apartment filled with voices. We ate in the living room with Amy on the sofa, and Yukon made the rounds from guest to guest scoring handouts. John Keeble slipped him a piece of buttered corn bread. "Shh," he said and held a finger up to his mustache.

When the food was gone from everyone's bowls and plates, Yukon curled on the floor in the middle of the crowd and fell asleep to the comforting sounds of close talk, a sound that must have also made its way into our baby's wet, dark world that tasted of casserole, broccoli and carrots, fruit salad, corn bread, and chili.

When Hannah's birthday did come, we took out the candle we'd first lit at her memorial service in Michigan. We put it in the window and lit it again, as we'd done on both her previous birthdays. I sat at the end of the sofa with Amy's head in my lap and we watched that steady flame.

At Amy's ultrasound appointment two days later, we learned that funneling was back in her cervix, which was open to within one centimeter of her top stitch. That much funneling still wasn't a cause for grave concern, Dr. Johnson told us, but she did say she thought it might make sense for Amy to go in the hospital before long. In the hospital Amy could wear a monitor belt around her belly for an hour every day to check for contractions.

"We have lots we can do to keep this baby inside," Dr. Johnson said. "But I think monitoring you daily for contractions is going to be important in letting us know what to do when. If we pick up contractions we can give you Indocin or Terbutaline, which counteract labor, and we can give you a course of steroids to speed the baby's lung development. We should talk about maybe doing the steroids anyway in the next week or two. And then we still have magnesium. You don't want to go on that unless you have to. It's not pleasant, but it usually works very well to halt contractions."

"Magnesium," Amy repeated. She sounded dazed.

"Yep, but only if you really need it. In here we could keep close tabs. Also, your room would be right down the hall from here so you won't have to come all the way from home twice a week for ultrasounds."

"I've been lying down all the time at home."

"She really has," I added.

"Oh Amy, I have absolutely no doubt in my mind you are. It's not about that. I have no doubt you're doing good bed rest at home. Here though the bathroom is ten feet from the bed, and you'd get monitored every morning for contractions and you'd have support staff for meals and glasses of water and any other need you might have while Jonathan's at work. The studies show that no matter how good you do at bed rest at home, moms in the hospital get further along before delivering."

Amy nodded. "How long would I be in for?"

"The rest of the pregnancy, probably. At thirty-five weeks we'd take the stitches out and let you go for a couple weeks more bed rest at home, until thirty-seven, when you could get up. But I don't expect us to get that far. I do think we'll get weeks yet, and I think we're likely to get the most time with you in the hospital."

We sat quietly, absorbing all she'd said, the words "in the hospital" hanging in the air.

"It's just something to think about over the next week or so," Dr. Johnson added. "No emergency. The good news here, guys, is you've got a 'go for baby.' That's what we call them at twenty-four weeks when they look as good as yours does. Pumpkin's one pound, six ounces. If we got no further this baby would have a 30 or 40 percent chance of surviving, and the odds just go up from here. You're going to get plenty further."

One week and two ultrasounds later, Amy's cervix was slightly more funneled. I packed a suitcase and we moved her into the hospital that afternoon. Right away we set about making the room feel like home. We knew she could be there for weeks or even months, so I brought pottery and the houseplants and herbs she was growing in the apartment and set them in the windowsill and on the shelves. I hauled up the used mini-fridge we'd bought for my office and stocked it with frozen tortellini, yogurt, milk, frozen corn and carrots, and veggie burgers so when Amy's food trays came from the cafeteria I could quickly fix myself a dinner in the nurses' station microwave and we could eat together.

There was a turquoise sofa in the room for me to sleep on, and to spruce that up, Amy had me bring our own throw pillows and a Mexican blanket with some turquoise in it. I also brought her her own pillows and a quilt, along with a stuffed penguin and a bear that Deb had given us for the baby. I set up a little table in the room as a study, with a row of the books I was teaching from along the back, so I could read student poems and prepare for class there.

I brought Amy the photo albums she'd been filling, and she paged through them and took out pictures for me to tack on the bulletin board across from her bed. One by one she handed me dozens of images of her and me, the cabin, Yukon, our families and friends in Spokane, Idaho, Pennsylvania, and Michigan. In one picture, Amy looked at the camera with the rail of a ferryboat and the Gulf of Alaska behind her. We were making our way back down from our summer in the far north, following our evolving dream of a homestead in the woods back to Idaho and the roughed-in cabin. Her eyes were the exact shade of the ocean behind her and she'd smiled at me as I took the picture.

I pushed thumbtacks into the corkboard above and below that photo. After all we'd been through, all we'd lost, and even as a prisoner in that hospital room, Amy still smiled like that often, facing straight toward me, her head level and her eyes wide open with a look that said, "I'm with you, Buddy. It's you and me."

She had me hang a calendar on that corkboard next to the photographs. That first night, when she got up to use the bathroom before going to sleep, she took a purple marker from her nightstand drawer and marked off Friday, March 17th, St. Patrick's Day, with an X. "Day one," she said and flashed me those green eyes before she closed the bathroom door.

But despite our increasing efforts at optimism, reality caved back in on us often. For all this struggle and sacrifice, Amy could still end up losing this baby, too. The unit Amy was housed on was Mother-Baby, where women and healthy newborns stayed after they left the delivery rooms. Every time I came and went I passed babies, babies through the nursery window, babies being pushed slowly down the hall in bassinets by mothers in bathrobes and fathers in rumpled T-shirts and jeans.

Dr. Johnson had said Amy could take one twenty-minute wheelchair ride a day around the hospital and grounds, and she'd said the first one should be a tour of the NICU, the Neonatal Intensive Care Unit. "There is a good chance Pumpkin will spend some time there and it helps make it less overwhelming if you've seen it first and met at least one of the staff."

The NICU was just upstairs from Mother-Baby, through double doors right next to the Labor and Delivery Unit. I hit the open button on the wall and we went in and explained to the nurse at the desk we'd been sent by Dr. Johnson for a tour. The nurse asked Amy how far along she was.

"Almost twenty-six weeks."

"Well, then, that's where we'll start. We've got a twenty-six weeker back there now." She stepped through a heavy glass door behind the desk and held it open for Amy's wheelchair.

In glass-walled rooms on either side of a central corridor lay babies in a variety of bassinets from simple ones, like those down on the regular nursery in Mother-Baby, to clear capsules around which orbited stacks of machines with computer keyboards and monitor screens displaying digital numbers and line graphs in orange and green and red. Miniature babies. Most had tubes up their noses and in their mouths and i.v. ports taped to their feet, and some had round heart monitors stuck to their chests. Some looked only a little smaller than the babies in the nursery downstairs. Others, the ones in the glass capsules with eye masks on their faces and plugged into all that equipment, had heads as small as tennis balls.

The nurse led us into one room and walked up beside just such a minuscule baby and whispered, "We keep it as quiet as we can in here and keep the lighting soft and indirect because too much stimulation can throw off their breathing and heart rate. This little guy's a twenty-six weeker."

The basinet was at eye level to Amy's wheelchair and inside, on a white fleece bedding, face down beside a photo of a His-panic-looking couple and a strand of rosary beads and cross, was the smallest human being I'd ever seen alive—though how he could be alive I couldn't fathom. His body was slen-der, without the folds of fat of a term infant, and his skin was a translucent reddish brown, his veins and arteries clearly visi-ble beneath. He couldn't have been much longer than a foot.

His body looked just like Hannah's.

"How many pounds?" I asked.

"One-seven," the nurse said.

"Can the parents hold him?" Amy asked, her voice steady though her eyes streamed with tears.

"Not yet. Their brains just can't handle it at this stage. We try to simulate the womb as much as possible."

"What's the tube up his nose for?"

"That's for feeding. It goes to his stomach. They just don't have the strength to suck this early. The ventilator tube in his mouth goes to the lungs."

One machine clicked softly each time the baby's back rose and fell. Beyond the baby, through a narrow opening between the almost closed vertical blinds on the window, the mountains at the Idaho boarder stood omnipresent along the horizon.

Amy stared into the bassinet.

"How about twenty-eight weeks?" I asked. "Dr. Johnson said twenty-eight is the next milestone for us."

"This little guy was twenty-nine," the nurse said, keeping her voice hushed and turning around to the bassinet behind her. "Twenty-nine and two days. He was born five days ago and is doing really good."

Fewer machines flanked this baby. He was certainly bigger. He lay on his back and his skin looked thicker, not so red and marbled with blood vessels. But tubes still disappeared into his mouth and nose, and an I.V. port was taped to his foot, too. His tiny chest was nearly eclipsed by the twin heart monitors stuck to it.

"We love twenty-nine weekers," the nurse said. "After twenty-eight or twenty-nine weeks the risk of cranial bleeding goes way down. Also, the vessels in their eyes are less likely to bleed. Their whole circulatory system is far less fragile. But the main thing is the lungs. Between twenty-six and about thirty weeks the lungs go through a period of great development. The lungs are the biggest issue for the little ones."

Breathing machines clicked and sighed all around us.

The nurse reached up into one of the cupboards and pulled down a box of tissue, which she handed to Amy. "Have you had steroid shots yet?"

"Not yet," Amy answered, wiping her eyes and nose dry. "Dr. Johnson said we'd talk about it this week."

"We see a real difference in how long it takes for them to breathe on their own if they've had them."

"We'll be sure to ask her," I said.

"Let me show you guys the twins," the nurse led us across the corridor to where a young, maybe even teenage woman with long, strawberry blond curls and Little Orphan Annie freckles splashed across her nose and cheeks sat in a rocking chair feeding a baby.

"This is Sarah," the nurse said.

Amy and I introduced ourselves and Sarah gave us a shy smile.

"Hi."

"Sarah volunteered for visiting bed-rest moms to meet her babies. Twin boys."

"This is Kyle," Sarah said and looked down at the baby in her arms. Then she craned her head toward the bassinet behind her. "That's Carter."

Both babies were small and had feeding tubes up their noses

to supplement the bottle, but they looked dramatically healthier than the others, almost like the term babies downstairs in the Mother-Baby Unit nursery. Kyle's blue eyes were open and staring up toward Sarah as she fed him.

"They're beautiful," Amy said.

"Thanks."

"How far along did you get?" I asked.

"Thirty-two weeks," she said proudly. "I was in here for the last five."

Kyle's sucking tapered off and his eyelids drooped.

"They've been born two weeks now," the nurse added. "So we refer to them as thirty-four weeks' gestation. Babies generally stay here until forty weeks' gestation—so these guys have a while yet, but they're doing great."

"How many pounds were they?"

"Three-ten and four-six."

Back downstairs in Amy's room the hushed tones we'd adopted in the NICU stayed with us all afternoon. But mostly we didn't talk at all. Amy wrote herself a note to ask Dr. Johnson about steroids and left it on her nightstand. I crawled in the narrow hospital bed beside her and we watched television into the evening. The top of the locust tree outside Amy's window was bare and black and the branches dividing into smaller and smaller and smaller branches made me think of those blood vessels under the twenty-six weeker's skin.

Amy fell asleep, and I drove home through the city night to feed and walk Yukon. From the streets of our neighborhood I could see the hospital on the hill above the downtown buildings. As Yukon marked a bush, I watched a strobe light on the belly of a helicopter get closer to the red lights outlining the hospital roof. The helicopter landed and the thumping sound of the rotors slowed and quieted to swishes.

When Dr. Johnson stopped in on her morning rounds, Amy asked her about the steroid injections. Dr. Johnson explained that, by speeding fetal lung development, steroids increase the survival rate for premature babies and decrease the risk of complications related to oxygen deprivation. But when we asked her about side effects as we always did with any intervention, she said the multiple doses women received until recently had been associated with an increased risk of learning disabilities that showed up in the babies later. The new protocol was only two doses, given twelve hours apart, which seemed to be enough for the benefits to the lungs but not enough to hinder brain development.

Still, Amy and I resisted the idea of medicating this baby we'd worked obsessively to keep healthy and safe in the womb. For months even before the baby was conceived, Amy hadn't consumed a milligram of artificial sweetener, flavor, or color. She'd eschewed caffeine, MSG, and anything with even a trace of alcohol in it, and now we had to consider sending down a chemical with a known track record of harming babies.

"Couldn't it be that the learning disabilities are too subtle, too mild to test for with the reduced doses, but still there?" I asked.

Dr. Johnson said the effects on the brain seemed to result from repeated exposure "the way many x-rays or cigarettes eventually damage tissue," while the benefit comes from a triggering effect. "It's a chemical signal that with just two or three exposures helps turn on the elasticity of the lungs."

Amy sighed. Her brow was a straight ridge across her forehead.

"But," Dr. Johnson added, "if you're worried I think we

could delay a decision. The steroids' trigger effect is relatively swift. They have to be administered while the baby's inside, but between the daily monitors and ultrasounds twice a week, I think we'd have several days' warning if you were going to deliver. We could buy some more time with magnesium even, enough to get the steroids on board and doing their job."

When Dr. Johnson had left and we were alone again, Amy rolled onto her side and stared out the window.

"Are you all right?" I asked. "That's good news. That we can wait on the steroids."

"This place drives me crazy," she said softly. "I just lie here. Day after fucking day. I hate my body for this. We might have to give the baby drugs because of my body."

"But your body's growing this baby."

"I keep thinking about Hannah. That tiny premie upstairs . . ."

"I know."

"Why couldn't we have done all this for her?"

"Because we didn't know. Nobody knew how weak your cervix was. Even Bowden said she thought you'd make it. This baby's chances are so good because of Hannah. We can do all this because of what we learned." I got into bed behind Amy and wrapped my arm around her. I put my hand on her belly.

"I love your body. It's got my baby inside."

Amy put her hand over mine. "I just want to do everything right this time."

"You are."

Amy rode the life raft of her hospital bed through the days that followed. And the days began to add up, each one marked off with a purple X on her calendar. Every morning a nurse wheeled a contraction monitor into Amy's room and strapped two sensors to her belly, one for contractions and the other for the baby's heart tones. We could listen to the heartbeat by turning a volume dial up. A line scrolled across the monitor screen indicating muscular activity in the uterus. Below, a paper ribbon spooled out a record of that line. Any long, gradual rising and falling bumps indicated contractions, and there were always a couple, ones Amy usually felt. We knew four or five an hour was normal—Braxton-Hicks they were called, and they trained the uterus muscles for their job ahead. It was a pattern, bumps at regular intervals every few minutes we watched for. Actually, I did most of the watching. Amy was content to mostly listen to the heart beating away as she read or wrote letters. I sat at my little study desk and made a show of preparing for class but glanced up at that line compulsively.

"I'll tell you if I feel one," Amy would say.

I didn't say that the reason she was hooked up was to detect any contractions she couldn't feel.

When the monitoring was finished and Dr. Johnson had visited on her rounds and read the strip and said it looked fine, I would walk the three blocks down to my building and hold office hours and teach. In the evening I'd walk back up to the hospital, where Amy'd quickly tell me about her afternoon—who'd called long distance, which nurses were on second shift—then ask me about mine. She wanted all the detail I could give her. Did I see John Keeble or any of the other faculty? How were the students? How was Anita, the secretary? Did the students give each other good comments on their poems? Was it as cold out as it looked?

Always the people I'd seen at school had asked about her and always I told her who and what they'd said to pass along. I made it a point to remember the specifics of every good wish. And I made it a point to remember the temperature on the digital Washington Mutual Bank sign I passed so I could tell her that, too.

If we had saved Amy's twenty-minute wheelchair privilege for the evening, we'd sometimes ride the elevator up to the top of the hospital's tower building and sit in front of the window. Below, the freeway from the east, the freeway that had been the last leg of my commute from Idaho throughout the fall, ran toward us like a river of light down from the mountains.

The cabin waited up in the headwaters of that river. It waited in the snow at the end of the snow-buried driveway as night got dark and we went back down to Amy's room and ate our dinners—Amy's on a cafeteria tray, mine in microwave-safe Tupperware bowls. Sometimes I rented a movie and borrowed a VCR cart from the nurses' station. Other nights we watched TV until the late news came on, then I'd drive home, check the message machine and mail, take Yukon for his night walk, and drive back to the hospital to sleep on that turquoise sofa beside Amy's bed.

On the first of April some of my students gave Amy a baby shower. She'd been in the hospital two weeks, on bed rest three months, and she'd made it to twenty-eight weeks. The baby was two pounds, nine ounces now, and at significantly less risk of long-term complications if it were delivered. My students decorated the room with crepe paper streamers and balloons and hung a banner that read "Baby Shower" on the wall. My aunt Marguerite drove down from the ranch and walked in carrying in her arms the handmade wooden cradle in which she'd rocked her own children.

People brought Thai food and pizza, wine, and sparkling grape juice for Amy. I got extra chairs from the nurses' station and we set up a buffet on my study table. As we ate, several conversations went at once until someone asked Amy what names we were considering.

Amy washed down a bite of pizza. "Well," she said, and everyone else stopped talking to listen. "For a boy Jonathan likes Finnian. I like it too."

The writers approved. A little splash of character. "Fin" one of them said to hear the sound of it.

"And for a girl I just love the name Anya."

"I'm growing to like it, too," I added. "It's the one girl's name that's really stuck."

"Anya is lovely," my aunt said.

There were more presents for the baby—a tiny winter hat with wooly ear flaps, miniature moccasins, bright baby blankets, and hooded baby towels. Anya's or Finnian's things. We stacked them high in the crib beside Amy's bed.

The weather turned warm and sunny and the snow melted away in town, though the mountains were still bone white against the blue sky. The locust tree outside Amy's window grew plump yellow-green buds. One of those April mornings, I drove home, got Yukon, and came back to the hospital. I parked on the street below Amy's window and left him in the pickup with, "You wanna see your girl? You miss her, don'tcha?"

His big polar bear head hung out the window and watched me disappear through the sliding doors. Minutes later the doors parted and there we were, Amy in her wheelchair with a blanket folded on what little remained of her lap, and me behind, pushing, with pillows tucked under my arms.

"Sweet Boogaloo!" she called out to him, and Yukon whined and barked his baritone woof and paced the front seat, rocking the truck. We wheeled out to the hospital lawn, and I spread the blanket beneath one of the budding trees there. Amy got

197

out of the chair and, with the slow deliberation of any mother in her last trimester of pregnancy, maneuvered herself down onto the blanket. I got Yukon out of the truck, clipped a leash on him, and he snapped my elbow straight tugging to get at Amy. He wagged the entire back half of his body as he bent over and licked her face.

Through laughter she told him, "Yes, Big Boy." She ran her fingers through his mane and scratched behind his ears. "Sweet Boogaloo. Okay, all the way down, Yuke." He lay down between us and panted away. "You don't like that lonely old apartment, do you?"

With Dr. Johnson's permission we would sometimes lie outside like that for two hours, Amy reading *What to Expect the First Year*, me poring over the sections of Homer's *Odyssey* I'd be teaching that night, and Yukon finally crashed out on his side and snoozing. People passed on the sidewalk and smiled at us with our blanket, books, pillows, and Amy's round belly, the wheelchair parked on the grass beside us.

On Monday of Amy's twenty-ninth week, Dr. Johnson left for a week of vacation. She was confident that everything would be fine while she was away; Amy's daily contraction monitoring had looked good, and the most recent ultrasounds were showing the cervix funneling hadn't progressed beyond about one centimeter above the top stitch. Still, I watched the contraction monitor even more closely than usual the next few days. In the absence of our guide and advocate, I gave up all pretense of reading, and while Amy clicked on the television and let *Good Morning America* chatter away, I mostly just looked at that yellow line.

Then, when Amy woke up on Thursday morning she felt

contractions off and on. She wrote down the times, and there were five or six an hour.

"Nothing to be overly concerned with yet," the nurse said as she wheeled the monitor into Amy's room. "Morning's an active time for contractions. Just keep on your left side and keep drinking lots of water and we'll see what the monitor says." She strapped the belt around Amy's middle, turned the machine on, and left.

Within a minute the line started the slow, uphill climb of a contraction.

"I can feel this one," Amy said as the line crested.

It flattened back down, and I poured her a glass of water, her fourth since she'd been awake. We were both watching that line now.

"Damn," Amy said when it went back up.

Over the course of a half-hour, the monitor showed five contractions, spread at roughly six minutes. An ultrasound scheduled for later that morning showed no cervical changes, good news, but the nurses put Amy back on the monitor that afternoon and the contractions still hadn't settled down.

The attending resident filling in for Dr. Johnson was Dr. Richards, a stout guy with a buzz cut who looked like a young Bruce Willis and walked through the door with a big "Hello folks. Got some rockin' and rollin' goin' on I hear." He told us that the contractions might go away on their own, especially since they hadn't caused the cervix to funnel any worse. On the other hand, he suggested we consider a course of Indocin to suppress them anyway, "just to get out ahead of this."

Amy explained that we'd hoped to avoid any drugs besides the Procardia she was already taking, and I asked Dr. Richards what he would do.

"You can't ask that," Amy said before he could respond. She was right. I knew Dr. Johnson wouldn't have answered, knew she wouldn't do anything to diminish our power, *Amy's* power. I realized that's what I was asking this young, energetic doctor to do, take the decision from her, but before I could stop him he answered, "My wife? No doubt I vote for the Indocin. Thirty weeks is still way early. The risks there really outweigh any downside to the Indocin, which there doesn't seem to be any. I'll let you guys talk about it and get back to you though."

When the door closed behind him I told Amy I was sorry I'd asked him what he would do.

"That's okay. I know you're just worried. I am, too." She hadn't had even a little of her power taken. "I guess we should do this," she said. "But the implications are so broad. It's a decision the baby will live with for the rest of its life."

"Hell," I said and walked over to the calendar. All those X's. Days she'd given away, bartered toward motherhood.

When Dr. Johnson returned on Monday, she told us we'd done the right thing. "Indocin's got a long track record. Plus the contractions went away. Good call, guys," she said and gave us that thumbs-up of hers.

We'd never know if the contractions would have gone away on their own or if the drug had stilled them, but either way the scare had passed as quickly as it had come. We were at thirty weeks' gestation.

Amy's mother flew out from Michigan to spend a week with us. She's small and athletic, like Amy, and she hit the ground in full grandmother mode. She walked Yukon every morning for me and did the laundry I'd let pile up in the apartment. She made Tupperware tubs full of tuna casserole and spaghetti pie for me to keep in the mini-fridge at the hospital. She gave Amy a baby quilt she'd been sewing for months—red and white checked with teddy bears. She borrowed the pickup and drove to the Baby Depot store, where she bought us a collapsible, nylon port-a-crib that breaks down to pack in a stuff sack, like a tent. "Perfect for you guys and all the traveling you do," she said when I had it set up in Amy's room next to the antique cradle my aunt had brought.

I folded the quilt in half and draped it over one side of the port-a-crib then sat down beside Amy's mom on the sofa.

"We're all ready now," Amy said.

"No rush," her mom said. "I've waited this long; I can wait a few more weeks."

She meant since the fall when we'd told her Amy was pregnant, we knew. But she'd also been waiting for three years, since Hannah. Like my parents, Amy's folks were still without grandchildren.

"Dr. Johnson said she thought we'd get to May, Mom, that this would be a May baby."

"Probably not a June bug," I added. "We'll have to call it May Fly."

"May Fly," Amy's mom repeated. "Did you ever think you'd make it that far?"

"We're not out of the woods yet, but now it's not so much about the baby surviving. It's about me keeping it inside long enough that it doesn't have to be on a ventilator, that there are no complications. That's what I'm hoping for. A short stay in the NICU."

"You two are so brave," her mom said. "Do you know how brave you are? To do all of this all over again after Hannah. Everything you've done for this baby . . ." She shook her head.

It seemed to me that what we were, what we'd become, wasn't as much courageous as grown-up. But I said nothing.

"I want this baby to know about Hannah," Amy said.

"Of course. Nobody will forget her. You couldn't have done this if not for her."

Amy put her a hand on either side of her belly. "That's what Jonathan's been saying, too. I guess it's true."

The sun shone the whole week of Amy's mother's visit. The locust outside the window bloomed with that gold Robert Frost called "Nature's first green," and Amy, her mom, and I could go outside most afternoons for our time with Yukon on the hospital lawn.

On the day she left I drove Amy's mother to the Spokane Airport. John Keeble had called Amy's room that morning to tell me I'd been renewed. I'd be teaching at the university another year. If the baby was out of the NICU and well enough to travel before the end of summer, Amy and I would take it back to Marquette for a visit, but after that we'd be coming back to live in the cabin.

Amy's mother rolled her window down and looked out at the mountains. "It's so beautiful here. If you two can't be in Marquette, this is a wonderful, wonderful place. And you've both done an amazing job getting this baby this far. I wish I could be here all the time, but it helps knowing you take such great care of Amy."

"She's doing all the real work," I said.

"She's really something, isn't she? She's already a great mother."

The baby did stay inside into May. Amy's birthday, May 7th, was coming up and the nurses started speculating that maybe the baby would be born then, which would be at thirty-three weeks. The ultrasound on May 4th showed the baby had wisps of hair, especially just above the nape. We could see the hair clearly in the photo the technician printed for us. But the ultrasound also showed that the funneling was deeper and wider, pulling at the stitches some, and Dr. Johnson told us we should revisit the issue of steroids.

"I just don't see us getting to thirty-five weeks, when steroids would no longer be advantageous," she said. "My concern now is that cervix of yours. I don't want those stitches to pull to the point where you could tear and do permanent damage. You could scar enough that future pregnancies wouldn't be possible. This baby may still need some time on the vent, but steroids could cut that down significantly. We really want good breathing. That's the key to the best outcome for Pumpkin."

More drugs, I thought. Those X's on the calendar should add up to more. They should be enough.

"You don't think we ought to push it another couple weeks?" Amy asked.

"I want to keep a real close eye on that cervix, like we have been, and if it puts any more pressure on those stitches we should take them out. If we had a course of steroids now, we could do that with a little less worry about the baby. But I want to make clear that there's no wrong choice here, guys. It's something for you to talk about, something for the two of you to decide. You've made it to almost the end of thirty-two weeks, past the point of greatest danger no matter what you do."

Amy and I did talk about the steroids. We got medical journals from the hospital library. We called upstairs to the NICU and spoke with one of the doctors there about his experience with thirty-two weekers who'd had steroids versus those who hadn't. He said that for boys it seemed more crucial than for girls, but you can usually tell with both genders which ones got them and which didn't.

It was after midnight when Amy finally pushed the nurse call button on her bed rail.

"Yes?" It was Susan, the frizzy-haired nurse who called us the hippies from the mountains and who said we were going to make the coolest parents. She'd been waiting for us to buzz her.

"I'm ready for my shot," Amy said into the air.

When Susan came in we apologized for taking so long to decide. She sat on Amy's bed and uncapped the syringe. "You health-food freaks. Of course you're gonna analyze something like this to death." Amy rolled up her sleeve as she had for the Indocin. "You get this in the backside, gal," Susan said. She gave Amy the shot and rubbed an alcohol swab on the spot. Then in a softer tone she said, "Sweeties, this was hard because you care about this baby. So many moms come though here and just do whatever the docs say, without even knowing what the shots and pills and procedures are even for. You're doing the best thing with the steroids, I swear, but what impresses the hell out of me, if you'll pardon my French, is the way you care."

I invited Susan to stay for a juice.

"What I'd really love, Hon, is a scotch, but we've got six moms and babies down from delivery with two more pairs on the way so I'd better stay sharp. Don't want to end up on *48 Hours with Dan Rather*: 'Drunk Nurse Switches Babes.'" She winked and left.

Amy and I were quiet. In a few seconds, if not already, those molecules would be crossing the placenta and catching a ride in the baby's blood up the umbilical cord. I turned out the light and crawled under my blanket on the sofa.

"I do care about this baby," Amy said in the dark.

On the morning of May 7, Amy's thirty-first birthday and the date when she turned thirty-three weeks pregnant, a dozen or so of the morning shift nurses and Dr. Johnson shuffled into Amy's room. They moved shoulder-to-shoulder, facing Amy's bed, like a chorus line in teddy-bear-print smocks and blue scrubs, shielding something Dr. Johnson held behind her back. Though it was Sunday, Theresa, one of Amy's ultrasound technicians, was there too, in her T-shirt and shorts, still flushed from her morning run.

"This probably isn't where you'd be today, if you had your preference, but we're sure glad you're with us," Theresa said and they all sang "Happy Birthday."

"We didn't get a chance to wrap this. It's been crazy around here," Dr. Johnson said as she brought a baby backpack out from behind her back and sat it on Amy's bed.

It was cobalt blue and very high-tech, with lots of zippered compartments for bottles and diapers.

"I love it!" Amy said.

"Ever since we first talked about having a baby Amy would point out people walking by with kids in these," I added.

We were still seven weeks shy of Amy's due date. Though they still generally needed weeks or months in the NICU, babies born at the point we'd made it to had almost as much chance of survival as those who reach full term. We knew that intellectually. But now here was this backpack that Dr. Johnson had conspired with the nurses to give Amy, a tangible sign of her confidence that we were going to have a living, healthy baby to sooner or later take home.

"You guys are going to have so much fun with Pumpkin," she said.

After hugs and thank-yous and promises to stop back before their shift was done, the nurses went back to work. Dr. Johnson asked Amy how the night had been and Amy said she'd had quite a bit of crampiness. Since Theresa was at the hospital anyway and the ultrasound room would be empty on Sunday, Dr. Johnson suggested we take an unscheduled look.

Theresa unlocked the ultrasound room and Dr. Johnson pushed Amy's wheelchair inside. Amy got out and climbed onto the table as she'd done more than two dozen times before and in seconds her cervix was on the screen.

"It's really pulling on the stitches, isn't it?" Amy asked.

"It sure is," Dr. Johnson said. She looked closely at the screen though the problem was obvious to all of us. The cervix was splayed wide on the inside, and barely held closed at the bottom by the stitches. "They've got to come out right away."

"Do you want me to give us a look at the baby?" Theresa asked.

"Yeah, we should take a quick look since we're here."

The baby was curled up, knees to chest, and sucking its fist.

"Heart rate 127," Theresa said. "This baby's sleeping."

"Getting good and rested up," Dr. Johnson added. "This pumpkin's got a little trip to take today, I think."

"You think it'll come right after you take the stitches out?" Amy asked without taking her eyes off the image of our sleeping baby.

"Well, I'm going to wear my rubber booties when I do it because I'm probably gonna get splashed."

"Vivid," I said with admiration.

"We'll stop the Procardia now, but there may be some delay in the labor as the effects wear off. Not much though, from the looks of that cervix. We'll take the stitches out up in the Delivery O.R., then take you over to a delivery room."

Theresa smiled. "Looks like those nurses who said this baby would have the same birthday as its mom were right," she said and pushed the button to print us one final ultrasound picture.

Amy thanked Theresa for coming in on her day off and Theresa wished Amy good luck. Dr. Johnson went off to scrub for the procedure, and I wheeled Amy back to her room so she could try to contact Deb, whom she'd invited to attend the delivery. Deb was flying into Spokane on her way back from the annual Idaho Domestic Violence Conference in Boise, so Amy left a message at the airport to page her and tell her to come straight to the hospital as soon as her plane landed.

Twenty minutes later Dr. Johnson dropped the first of Amy's stitches into a pan, then held up the second, top stitch with a hemostat and announced, "There it is." It was maybe three inches long—a green monofilament strand that looked exactly like dry-fly fishing line. She turned it in the air and we all studied it. "You and this stitch both did your jobs beautifully, Amy. You've dilated to two centimeters already."

Amy was moved down the hall from the O.R. to a birthing room where her bed faced a wall of windows filled with mountains. "Thought you might want to be able to look out and see home," Dr. Johnson said. Because Amy had been previously diagnosed as a carrier of beta strep, Dr. Johnson ordered an I.V. drip of antibiotics to prevent the bacteria from passing to the baby during delivery. Once again this baby would benefit from what we learned from Hannah.

After the labor and delivery nurse had inserted the port in Amy's wrist and hung the drip bag, she strapped a contraction monitor around Amy's belly. "You'll likely have contractions right away from the muscle irritation of having the stitches out," Dr. Johnson said. "Let's just wait and see what develops. You shouldn't eat anything; what goes down often comes up during labor. When the baby gets close, I'll call one of the doctors over from the NICU."

"Will I get to hold it?" Amy asked.

"I hope so. We'll try to do that, at least for a little while. Pretty quickly, though, Pumpkin will probably have to head down to the NICU."

Amy looked right into my eyes and said, "Don't leave the baby. Not for one second."

"I won't." I bent over to hug her but she held her hands against my shoulders to stop me.

"I'm serious. Don't stay with me. Promise me you'll go with the baby and stay there. Don't let the baby out of your sight for one second." She turned toward Dr. Johnson. "He's allowed to do that, isn't he?"

"He absolutely is allowed to do that."

"I swear," I said.

When the nurse and Dr. Johnson left I got in bed beside Amy. "When the baby comes I'm going to hold it up to those windows so it can see Idaho," I said.

"Not till after I hold it you won't!"

"That's what I meant."

"They can only see a couple of inches in front of their faces at first."

"I don't care."

"You goof," Amy nuzzled her head into the crook of my arm. "I just hope the baby can stay with us awhile. I'm going to miss it so much."

The monitor showed regular contractions right away, but for over an hour Amy felt only mild tightness in her belly, not full-blown labor pains, and her water didn't break. Deb showed up, knocking softly on the door and stepping in with "No baby yet?" She was out of breath, her pantsuit was rumpled, and her hair was disheveled, but she asked how Amy was doing.

"Starving. They aren't letting me eat because they don't want me to puke."

"That's delightful. Look at you two, making yourselves quite comfortable."

"It's so good to see you."

"Happy Birthday, kid," Deb said. "My heart really kicked in when I heard my name over the airport loudspeakers. The operator just said to get here."

"Sorry." I said, "but it's good to have you here." And it was. Deb was our witness, she'd seen us struggle toward parenthood the entire time we'd known her, and it was fitting that she would be here now.

Only, as the three of us wore the day into evening talking, now didn't seem to be the baby's time. The contractions tapered off some, and when Dr. Johnson stopped in to check, Amy's cervix was still only two centimeters.

"The head's right there, though, right in position. Let's just stay in this holding pattern and see. Meanwhile, I think it's safe for you to eat a little something, which is good because the second shift nurses from downstairs are just outside this door with pizza and birthday cake. I'm going home but I live seven minutes from here, and I'll have the nurses' station call me if there are any developments."

The nurses brought in the food and Amy ate, closing her eyes and humming "Mmm" after each of the first few bites. They left soon to get back to work and Deb drove to our apartment to walk Yukon. By the time she returned an hour later, Amy's contractions had stopped almost altogether and the nurse had checked her cervix and found it still only two centimeters dilated.

"Well," Deb said with a shrug. "Babies come when babies want to come."

"Unless we get surprised, it won't be born on my birthday after all," Amy added.

The nurse returned a short time later and said Dr. Johnson had called and she wanted Amy to stay up in the delivery room one more hour. By then it would have been twelve hours since the stitches came out, and if she still wasn't having regular contractions, she could go back downstairs, where she could start the Procardia again.

It was dark outside and Deb had a two-hour drive to her place up on the Clark Fork River, so Amy sent her home with a hug and tried to apologize for the false alarm, but Deb stopped her. "Don't you dare," she scolded. "I'm honored that you two want me here when it comes. Call me if you go back into labor after all, on my cell phone if I'm not home yet. Otherwise, get some sleep tonight. You both look exhausted."

Amy didn't go back into labor. When we finally returned to her room on Mother-Baby, it had the familiarity of home. Someone had made up Amy's bed, folded our throw blanket neatly on the back of the sofa, and placed the baby backpack in the wooden cradle with the shower gifts. Amy got in under the covers, and I collapsed on the sofa and pulled the throw over me.

Every day for a week we woke up thinking that this would be the day. Dr. Johnson was as surprised as we were that the baby didn't come and told us that a mom with a weak cervix rarely stays pregnant long once her stitches are taken out.

"One more week and you'll be at thirty-five," she said. "We'll send you home then if you still haven't delivered. Then, after a week of bed rest there we'll stop the Procardia and you'll be a free woman. Don't plan on it, though. I'm just pleased with every day we get now. At this point every day with this baby inside tends to cut two days off the NICU stay."

When we were alone, Amy confided in me that her goal now was a baby that comes home from the hospital with us. "I'm getting greedy, I know, but we're this close. I can't believe we're this close, but we are."

The leaves on the locust out Amy's window offered themselves up in full. They shivered waxy and green in the mid-May sun and wind. I bought Amy a green fleece coat for Mother's Day and signed the card "From Anya/Finnian—still in utero."

Then, on May 21st, nine weeks and two days after she'd been admitted, Amy was discharged. Amazingly, she was still only two centimeters dilated, and Dr. Johnson speculated that the Procardia and bed rest had been enough to keep labor from progressing. One more week of both at home was all that remained. I took down the pictures and the calendar with all those days Xed out. I boxed up the pottery and all the stuffed animals and baby outfits and blankets. I packed Amy's clothes and broke down the port-a-crib and stuffed it in its stuff sack. When I had all of that and the cradle, baby backpack, and other presents out in the truck, I came for Amy with a wheelchair.

"It looks like a hospital room again," she said.

"Will you miss it?"

"Hell no." She got out of bed and into the wheelchair and I rolled her out the door.

We said good-bye to the nurses at the station, each of whom hugged us both and said they were already fighting over who got to take care of Amy when she came back after her delivery.

When Amy stepped through the door of our apartment, Yukon turned himself in circles in front of her and whined with joy. He joined her in our bed and didn't leave her side the rest of her first day home.

We resumed our prehospital routine. For a week Amy reclined on the sofa or in bed, reading books, writing letters, or talking on the phone, and I fixed meals for her to microwave, rushed off to class, called her on my breaks, and rushed back home to join her for some evening television or a video.

Then, on the morning of May 28th, Amy sat up, slipped her feet into her sneakers (which I tied since she could no longer reach her feet), and walked outside. She had been lying down for twenty-one weeks.

Like an astronaut returning from space, her legs were weak at first so she kept her trips short—to the grocery store for milk and cereal or two blocks to the park, stopping frequently to smell rose blossoms and watch parents push children on the swings. We went to movies and restaurants, where waitresses and people at neighboring tables smiled at us. We went to baby clothes stores and picked out tiny T-shirts and bibs. I took pictures of Amy standing, surrounded by lilacs, hands on her belly. For a small window of time, we lived like any expectant couple in their last days alone.

And we were grateful beyond any gratitude we'd known, not only for the baby we were expecting, but also for the present, for all these current moments in which Amy was lovely and pregnant and we were free to go out on the town, to simply step out to the sidewalk. Grateful for each other. Here we were on the brink, at the very border of what-comes-next, having lived so much of our lives dreaming and building and struggling toward one beautiful future or another, and we were perfectly happy to be right where we were. Knowing us, I knew we'd make more plans, maybe an addition on the cabin, maybe another cabin back in Michigan to stay in when we visit there. Daydreaming seems to be congenital with us. But we'd learned that the everyday can be a kind of dream, too. I could think of nothing more important for a parent to know.

On the last day of May the ultrasound showed that the baby was six pounds, two ounces. Healthy in every way. "It'll be a June bug after all," Amy said. Her cervix was still only two and a half centimeters dilated and Dr. Johnson told us that perhaps the long-term pressure on the stitches had caused a tough ring of tissue to develop, which was just enough to check further dilation.

"At any rate, if you'd told me back in March that we'd get to June, I wouldn't have believed it. You're totally out of the woods now, guys. Thirty-six and a half weeks. Any baby born at thirty-seven or later we count as full term." She added that, without the Procardia or bed rest, Amy would certainly deliver soon and in the meantime we ought to keep enjoying ourselves.

"No problem," I told her.

After another week of restaurants, parks, movies, and baby clothes shopping, we went back to Dr. Johnson, and this time, when she was done feeling Amy's cervix, she asked if we were ready to have this baby.

"You're four centimeters."

"I am?" Amy sat up.

"Four centimeters. And the head's right there, ready to go. This is it, guys. If you want to go home and pack a suitcase, you can come back to Labor and Delivery in an hour or so. You know where that is. I'll call up and see if I can get you the room you had before, with the Idaho view."

It turned out that room was occupied, and when we returned to the hospital we were shown another room around the corner and down the hall. This room was almost directly above Amy's old, Mother-Baby room. The window didn't face mountains, but it did overlook the top of the tree that had been Amy's companion for nine weeks.

"I'm glad it's the first tree the baby will see," she said.

"It's a great tree."

After Amy was changed into a gown and started on an I.V. drip of the beta strep–killing antibiotics, Dr. Johnson came in, wheeled a stool over beside Amy's bed, and said, "I'm thinking maybe we should talk about breaking your bag of waters. This baby's delivery is inevitable in the next couple days and there is no real advantage to waiting. Breaking the waters will get full-blown labor started quicker and maybe over quicker. You seem strong and well-rested now. What do you think?"

"I'm ready to have this baby," Amy said. "If there's no advantage to waiting, I think that would be the best thing. I just don't want to take any drugs other than these antibiotics. Nothing to speed up labor, no pain medicine."

"Then that's what we'll shoot for. Breaking your waters now, when you feel good, will help with that."

It was a simple procedure. After so many months of helping Amy keep this baby inside, Dr. Johnson used a small, plastic hook to snag, then pull a tear open in the amniotic sac. Only a small amount of fluid came. "The rest is behind Pumpkin. It will all come later, trust me," Dr. Johnson said as she wheeled her stool back away from Amy's bed and took her gloves off. "Like last time, I'd recommend no food, but otherwise I'd say feel free to walk around or take a bath. No need for the monitor right now. I'll check back with you in a while."

When Dr. Johnson left, Amy called Deb at the shelter in Sandpoint and told her the baby was coming. "This time I promise," she said, and Deb said she'd start down as soon as she could find a staff member to cover for her.

The contractions began almost right away, but Amy wanted to take a walk anyway. "To help them along," she said, climbing out of bed and putting on her bathrobe. We walked the halls of the third floor, moving slowly, Amy holding the rail on the wall with one hand and holding my hand with the other. She'd stop every couple minutes and grip my hand.

"Now *these* are contractions," she said, then eased her grip.

"Do you want to go back?"

"No. If this will help get the baby here quicker, let's keep walking."

We wandered the floor, covering a few feet at a time between contractions, until we came to the big, blue doors with "Neonatal Intensive Care Unit" written across them in white letters. A smaller sign below told parents to please check in at the nurses' station before visiting.

There was nothing to say. We stood there a moment and turned around.

Just ninety minutes later Amy was standing in the bathroom, naked, her arms around my neck and her knees buckling under her. I held her up under her arms; she was wet, stepping out of the bathtub when the contraction crested.

"Buddy, I'm afraid. Oh God!" she screamed. "I don't know what to *do*."

"Just get this one behind you."

"Are you okay in there?" A nurse knocked on the door. "You're making me nervous, Sweetheart. Come on out so you don't deliver this baby on the tile floor."

"Ow! Oh, ow! It hurts!"

"Get it over and you never have to do this contraction again," I said. "It's one you never have to do again."

Amy looked up and her eyes shot fire into mine. "Stop saying that!"

"Okay. I'm sorry. You're doing so good, though."

Another knock on the door. "Amy?" It was Dr. Johnson.

"We're okay. We're coming," I answered.

"I think I should check your cervix."

"We'll be right out."

"Help me put this on," Amy said and reached up for her gown on the door hook.

"I'll dry you off first." I grabbed a towel off the rack.

"Hurry," she said. "Before another one comes."

I got her dry and in her gown and back into bed just before another contraction hit.

"Oh Buddy, it hurts so bad. I can't take it. I need something. I need to take something. Ow! Oh, God!"

"Just get through this one and we'll have Dr. Johnson check you. You're doing terrific."

When the contraction subsided, Dr. Johnson checked and said, "You're almost there. Eight and a half centimeters, one and a half to go. I'm going to get my scrubs on and I'll be back in a few minutes. Meanwhile, I want you to wear this so we can see how Pumpkin's holding up." She strapped a monitor belt around Amy.

Amy gave a weak smile. "I'm close?"

"Very."

"God this hurts, Bud. I had no idea. I feel like I'm going to split open."

When Dr. Johnson returned she looked at the monitor and said, "Looks like Babe's doin' just fine. Strong heart rate." She checked Amy again. Ten centimeters. "You can push now, but just during the contractions."

Amy nodded. She was drenched in sweat, her dark bangs plastered against her pale forehead, and her eyes were closed.

A nurse wheeled in a tray with a blue linen bundle on top. She unfolded the linen to reveal rows of steel instruments; then she reached up and pulled a cord above Amy's bed. An exam light swung down from a trapdoor. The nurse left and returned again, this time pushing a tray with a scale on it.

"I'm getting another one," Amy said.

"Hold your knees if you want to, and Jonathan and I will help." Again, Amy nodded. Dr. Johnson placed a hand under one of Amy's knees and held it up, then told me to do the same on my side.

"Is this better, Amy?"

Another nod, then Amy's face flushed purple and tightened like a fist. "Oh! Oh!" She clenched her jaw and shut her eyes and moaned.

"Go ahead and push through it." Dr. Johnson used her free hand to stroke back Amy's bangs. "That's it! That's a good one."

"You're doing great!" the nurse said.

In a few seconds it passed and Amy collapsed as if unconscious. We lowered her legs.

"Amy," Dr. Johnson said, "Next time we'll start counting when the contraction comes. We'll start counting and you push till we get to ten. Okay?"

"Till you get to ten," Amy said from a hundred miles away. I looked outside. A new rain speckled the window.

Amy opened her eyes. "Is Deb here? Don't let them keep her out."

"There's no one out in the hall," the nurse said, "but I'll tell the desk to let her through when she comes."

Amy rolled her head to see the fetal heart monitor screen. "Is the baby okay?"

"Doing great! Just perfect," Dr. Johnson gave her trademark thumbs-up. I went in the bathroom and ran warm water on a washcloth, came back out, and held it to Amy's forehead.

"Feels good," she said.

For an hour Amy pushed, and she seemed to die down into the bed during the brief intervals between contractions. She still hadn't taken anything for the pain, and she'd said nothing more about needing something. She'd breathe hard but was otherwise still as the blood drained from her face. Then she'd start to huff and she'd sit up and grab her knees and pull and grunt as I counted. When she'd finished she'd collapse again, and the nurse would tell her to breathe deep, cleansing breaths.

Dr. Johnson moved from the side of the bed, asked the nurse to take over holding up Amy's knee, and sat down on the stool between Amy's feet.

The next contraction came and I counted again, "One, two, three."

"I can see a head!"

"Four, five, six."

Amy's eyelids were vises.

"That's it, Amy!" Dr. Johnson bounced on her toes. "That's it! Push, Amy, push!" She was bouncing. How many hundreds of babies had she delivered, and she was bouncing.

"Seven, eight, nine, and ten!"

"Great, great job, Amy, great job!"

"You saw the head?" Amy asked in one breath.

"Sure did! I still can."

Dr. Johnson stood up and held her arm out toward Amy. "Look, I've got goose bumps." She looked at me. "Come see the head, Dad." I moved down next to her and saw a circle of scalp, silvery wet and swirled with hair.

Amy propped herself up on her elbows, her eyes searching mine. "Do you see it?"

"There is a head."

She closed her eyes and collapsed again.

Deb walked through the door. "Hi," she whispered to me.

"Just in time," I said as Amy gasped in pain. I held up her knee and got my face down close to hers.

"One, and two, and three . . ."

Deb came over to Amy's other side and, when the contraction ended and Amy had caught her breath, said, "You poor kid, what in the hell are these people doing to you?"

"I'm having the baby, Deb."

"There's no doubt about that."

"Oh God!"

And that quickly Amy was back inside another contraction. "One, two, three . . ." The rain was coming down now as drops ran to streaks down the glass.

The time between contractions got shorter and more of the crown of the baby's head came into view until, finally, Dr. Johnson told Amy to keep pushing even between contractions as much as she could.

"This is it!" She shouted. "Keep the pressure on! That's great! Keep pushing, Amy!" She was bouncing up on her toes again. "You're going to get this baby out now."

At each contraction Amy would rock the top half of her body forward and bear down, but now when it passed she wouldn't ease off. She'd scream out then breathe hard and lean back, her face holding its intensity.

"I want you to take that scream and send it down toward the baby. Keep it in and make it a push, all the focus *down*."

"I love you," I said from Amy's other side.

"I love you, too," she grunted and rocked back up. The tendons in her neck tightened. Her blood vessels rose under her skin. She pushed.

"The head's here!" Dr. Johnson announced and the nurse reached into a drawer beside the bed and got out a turkey baster–type bulb, which she handed to Dr. Johnson. I leaned over to look and saw the back of the baby's head out, Dr. Johnson reaching under, to the face, with the bulb to suction fluid from the nostrils.

"Push, Amy, push this baby!" Dr. Johnson shouted. She reached a finger in under one shoulder and eased it out.

Amy made the slightest, closed-mouth cry and drove her scream down into herself, to the baby, and the baby was born.

The baby was born.

The baby was born in a gush of clear liquid, blood, and

mucus. Dr. Johnson turned the baby's face up and those arms sprung wide like the arms of a conductor opening to embrace the music in the instant before it starts.

A girl. "It's a girl!" I said.

"It is?" Amy's eyes opened. "It is?" She craned her neck to look.

"A beautiful little girl." Dr. Johnson said and quickly suctioned more fluid from the nostrils and mouth.

The baby let out a couple of squawks—sweet squawks from strong lungs.

"Dad, why don't you take this little girl up to her mama," Dr. Johnson said.

The baby moved again, arching her back and bending her legs a little at the knees. Then she moved again. And again. And she kept on moving.

I reached down to her, slid one hand under her shoulders, neck, and head, and the other hand under her bottom and lifted her. Her eyes stayed closed and she squawked some more as I carried her along the length of her mother's body to her mother's arms.

"Hi, baby. Hi, my baby. My baby." Amy lay back with the baby high on her chest, inches from her face. She looked up at Dr. Johnson, then the nurse and Deb. "Her name is Anya." She looked at the baby. "Anya."

"Hi, Anya," the nurse said and stroked the back of her head.

"Could you help untie the neck of my gown?" Amy said to the nurse. "I want to hold her on my skin."

"The luckiest baby in the world," Deb said. She backed away from Amy's side and sank down in a chair by the window.

Dr. Johnson clamped off the translucent, rubbery umbilical cord with two yellow clamps. She handed me a pair of scissors and pointed. "Right between the two," she said and I cut.

A little blood drained from the ends and Anya belonged to the world.

Her nose was very slightly upturned, as was her upper lip. Her cheeks were round. She looked like Hannah. Except she was a full-size baby, tiny though she was, and she had more hair, fine, coppery hair, wet hair, and her skin was getting lighter by the moment, from blue to pink as she drank breath after breath of air.

Her eyelids parted for the first time, just enough to show her blue irises, then closed.

"Hi, baby. I'm here," Amy whispered and the eyelids opened wider and stayed open.

I leaned in close to the two of them. "That's your mom." I kissed Amy's salty-wet forehead. "I'm your dad."

"Amy, I need you to push some more for the placenta," Dr. Johnson said. "Just a nice constant pressure is fine."

"Okay."

"Whenever you're ready I'll weigh her and give her a quick check-over," the nurse said. "I promise I'll give her right back."

"Not quite yet." Anya's eyes were drifting over Amy's face.

"You might have a tough time borrowing this one from her mama," Deb said from her chair.

The nurse smiled. "I'll stay within fifteen feet of the bed at all times."

"Soon," Amy said without taking her eyes off Anya. I crouched close to them and rested my hand on Anya's back, which rose and fell in strong, constant waves. "Soon."

When Amy eventually let the nurse weigh and measure Anya, we learned that she was six pounds, nine ounces, and nineteen and a half inches long. The nurse wrote these numbers down then said aloud, "Born at 1:25 p.m., June 8th, Anya Campbell Howko-Johnson. One healthy baby."

As I hovered beside, the nurse put a tall, purple and pink striped cap on Anya's head and wrapped a blanket around her. "The white, Crisco-like stuff is vernix." She pointed to it in the folds of Anya's skin. It was also on both my hands. "It's like cold cream. It keeps their skin smooth even though they're soaking in fluid. Babies usually lose it at forty weeks, so they come out more wrinkled than this smooth little girl."

Amy finished delivering the placenta, and I brought Anya to her again.

"Back to your mom, Little Shmo," I said. She was still wide-eyed and alert and she stayed that way until she was at Amy's breast. When Amy held her there Anya's eyes closed and her mouth opened like a little bird's. With her mouth opened like that she shook her head back and forth a couple of times then closed her lips around Amy's nipple.

She held her tiny fists up to either side of her head and the jaw muscles that ran up to her temple flexed as she sucked her mother's milk.

Anya saw the cabin for the first time when she was two weeks old. I was in the bathroom, brushing tarry glue into a pipe elbow then pushing in a black plastic pipe to complete the drain line for the bathtub, which was finally in place. I could hear talking and rips from the hacksaw outside where John Keeble and my uncle Steve were measuring and cutting more drain pipe for the toilet and bathroom and kitchen sinks. John had come up from Spokane with me early in the morning and Steve had joined us. I'd been determined to get the tub installed before Amy and Anya and Claire Keeble showed up with lunch. And now the rips of the handsaw stopped and I heard the slow labor of a car engine coming up the steep road.

I stepped out into the sunlight as our 4Runner emerged

through the trees. In our absence the grass and daisies had grown up so that walking the path from the cabin to where Amy parked beside John's pickup was like wading through thigh-deep water. I let my fingertips skim the surface.

Amy and Claire got out. "Hi, Bud. I brought you your baby," Amy said with a kiss.

"I hope so."

The black eyes that had appeared on Amy's face the day after the delivery were fading, but there were still purple, quarter-moon bruises above both cheeks, and the outer corner of her left eye was still red with burst vessels. Battle wounds.

She opened the back door and Yukon jumped down. He ran over to me for a quick pat then trotted off, head above the daisies, toward the cabin. Amy leaned in to get Anya from her car seat.

"Sorry we're late," Claire said. She hugged me with one arm and gave the cooler in her hand a little lift. "Are you boys famished?"

"You're right on time. We just put the tub in."

Amy reappeared with Anya in her arms. "The tub? You did?"

"Just put it in."

"Hellooooo Anya!" Steve called from the deck.

"I want to see it," Amy said.

"Okay, the glue fumes are pretty strong in there though. Better let me hold her."

"Sly," Amy said and handed Anya to me. She reached back into the truck for the diaper bag and a jug of water. She pushed the door closed with her foot. "Won't need to pack water much longer, I guess."

"Nope."

Anya had on a one-piece outfit, pastel green with Big Bird's face embroidered on the chest. She stretched, arching her back and pushing her head against my hand, closed her eyes, and opened her mouth in a wide, long yawn. Amy kissed her cheek. "This is your home, Baby June Bug."

Steve and John brought chairs onto the deck and we all sat there eating our tuna sandwiches and grapes and passing around a water jug. Yukon slept on his side in the middle of us. John tilted back his straw cowboy hat, closed his eyes, and let the sun shine on his face.

"Remind you of the old times, Keeble?" Claire asked John. "Babies and building?"

"It's good." He smiled slightly beneath his mustache.

A chickadee peep-peeped in the heat.

"I was thinking the same thing," Steve said. "We built our house when our kids were small. Tools and sawdust all over the place."

"How it should be," Amy said. "At least for a little while."

I propped my boot heels against a chopping block and held Anya slightly elevated on my lap, her head cupped in my palm. Down in the Spokane apartment Amy and I had boxed up our belongings. We'd be moving everything back to the cabin as soon as the plumbing work was done. Then we'd be off to Michigan for a long visit to introduce our parents to their granddaughter. When we returned in late summer, there would be more work—a woodshed to build and firewood to cut and haul and chop between my trips down to Spokane three days a week to teach. I'd have to put a rail at the edge of the loft before Anya reached crawling age. We would keep moving forward as we had all along. But there was no hurry.

I leaned down close to Anya's face and saw in the sphere of her eyes my own silhouette, the reflection of the fir and aspen trees and the peak of the cabin roof above me. It was the world Hannah never knew. But it was her legacy. Anya didn't know it and it will be years before we tell her, but the life she opened her eyes to was the gift her sister left behind.

IN THE AMERICAN LIVES SERIES

Fault Line
by Laurie Alberts

Pieces from Life's Crazy Quilt
by Marvin V. Arnett

Hannah and the Mountain:
Notes toward a Wilderness Fatherhood
by Jonathan Johnson

Local Wonders: Seasons in the Bohemian Alps
by Ted Kooser

Turning Bones
by Lee Martin

Thoughts from a Queen-Sized Bed
by Mimi Schwartz

Gang of One: Memoirs of a Red Guard
by Fan Shen

Scraping By in the Big Eighties
by Natalia Rachel Singer

In the Shadow of Memory
by Floyd Skloot

Secret Frequencies: A New York Education
by John Skoyles

Phantom Limb
by Janet Sternburg